CHRISTIAN IDENTITY
in a POSTMODERN AGE

Celebrating the Legacies of

KARL RAHNER

and

BERNARD LONERGAN

Edited by Declan Marmion

VERITAS

First published 2005 by
Veritas Publications
7/8 Lower Abbey Street
Dublin 1
Ireland
Email publications@veritas.ie
Website www.veritas.ie

ISBN 1 85390 808 8

A catalogue record for this book
is available from the British Library.

Printed in the Republic of Ireland
by The Leinster Leader

Veritas books are printed on paper made from the wood pulp of managed
forests. For every tree felled, at least one tree is planted, thereby renewing
natural resources.

Table of Contents

Contributors

Eamonn Conway is Head of the Department of Theology & Religious Studies at Mary Immaculate College, University of Limerick. He has edited *Technology & Transcendence*, Dublin: Columba Press, 2003; *Child Sexual Abuse and the Catholic Church – Towards a Pastoral Response*, Dublin: Columba Press, 1999; *The Splintered Heart: Conversations with a Church in Crisis*, Dublin: Veritas, 1998; *Twin Pulpits: Media and Church in Ireland*, Dublin: Veritas, 1997, and is author of *The Anonymous Christian – A Relativised Christianity? An Evaluation of Hans Urs von Balthasar's criticisms of Karl Rahner*, Frankfurt: Peter Lang, 1993. His current research interests include the ecclesial structural issues raised by the child sexual abuse crisis in the Catholic Church, the impact of technology on Christian spirituality.

Cynthia S. W. Crysdale is an Associate Professor and Associate Dean in the School of Theology and Religious Studies at the Catholic University of America. Her doctoral work focused on Bernard Lonergan's notion of moral development and she continues to work in the areas of ethics, feminism, and religion and culture. She is the editor of *Lonergan and Feminism*, Toronto: University of Toronto Press,

1994 and author of *Embracing Travail: Retrieving the Cross Today*, New York: Continuum, 2001. Recently she has become involved in science and religion conversations, and is particularly interested in developing Lonergan's notion of emergent probability.

Philip Endean, SJ, was for some years on the staff of Heythrop College, University of London, and is now Tutor in Theology at Campion Hall, Oxford, while also acting as Editor of *The Way*. He has published several articles, notably on Ignatian topics, and *Karl Rahner and Ignatian Spirituality*, Oxford: Oxford University Press, 2001.

Michael Paul Gallagher, SJ, is an Irish Jesuit. He was lecturer in Modern English and American Literature at University College, Dublin for 20 years and is now Professor of Fundamental Theology at the Gregorian University Rome, with a specialisation in 'frontier questions'. His most recent books include: *The Human Poetry of Faith*, New York: Paulist Press, 2003, and *Clashing Symbols: An Introduction to Faith and Culture* revised and enlarged edition, New York: Paulist Press, 2003.

Linda Hogan is lecturer at the Irish School of Ecumenics, Trinity College Dublin. She is the author of *From Women's Experience to Feminist Theology*, Sheffield: Sheffield Academic Press, 1995 and *Confronting the Truth, Conscience in the Catholic Tradition*, New York, Paulist Press, 2000. She is currently working on the appropriation of human rights categories in Christian ethics.

Dermot A. Lane is President of Mater Dei Institute of Education, a College of Dublin City University, and an occasional lecturer in Milltown Institute of Theology and Philosophy. He is author of *The Experience of God: An Invitation to Do Theology*, Dublin: Veritas, 2003 (revised and expanded edition) and editor of *Catholic Theology Facing the Future: Historical Perspectives*, Dublin: Veritas/New York, Paulist, 2003. His current research interests are focused on the roles of anthropology, memory and imagination in the reconstruction of theology for interreligious dialogue.

Declan Marmion, SM, is Lecturer in Systematic Theology at the Milltown Institute of Philosophy and Theology, Dublin. He is author of *A Spirituality of Everyday Faith: A Theological Investigation of the Notion of Spirituality in Karl Rahner*, Louvain Theological & Pastoral Monographs 23, Louvain: Peeters/Eerdmans, 1998 and co-editor of *The Cambridge Companion to Karl Rahner*, Cambridge: Cambridge University Press, 2005. Research interests include the theology of Karl Rahner and contemporary trinitarian theology.

William Mathews, SJ, has been lecturing in philosophy at the Milltown Institute of Philosophy and Theology, Dublin since 1980. He is the author of *Lonergan's Quest, A Study of Desire in the Authoring of Insight*, Toronto: University of Toronto Press, forthcoming, and has published in *Milltown Studies*, *Method: Journal of Lonergan Studies*, and *Lonergan Workshop* (Boston College). His research interests include philosophical anthropology and the interrelation between philosophy and biography.

Michael McCabe, SMA, has been Dean of Studies and Professor of Systematic Theology, St Paul's College-Seminary, Liberia, and from 1996-2001 Professor in Mission Studies at the Kimmage Mission Institute. His doctoral thesis

(1981) was entitled *The Role of Eschatology in the Writings of Reinhold Niebuhr and Its Relevance to His Socio-Political Critique*. He is a member of the International Association of Catholic Missiologists and of the British and Irish Association of Mission Studies.

Raymond Moloney, SJ, is Emeritus Professor of Systematic Theology in the Milltown Institute of Philosophy and Theology, Dublin. He is author of *The Knowledge of Christ*, London/New York: Continuum, 1999, a theological study of Christ's knowledge and consciousness.

Hilary Mooney is Privatdozentin (Dogmatics, History of Dogma, History of Theology) at the Albert-Ludwigs-Universität Freiburg where she teaches Early Church History and Patrology. Her doctoral dissertation focused on the aesthetics of Bernard Lonergan and she is currently preparing a study of the theology of Johannes Scottus Eriugena for publication.

Abbreviations

Bernard Lonergan
Method: *Method in Theology*. London: Darton, Longman & Todd, 1972.

C: *Collection*: *Papers by Bernard Lonergan, SJ.* Ed. Frederick E. Crowe, New York: Herder and Herder, 1967.

2*C*: *A Second Collection*. Ed. William Ryan and Bernard Tyrrell, London: Darton, Longman and Todd, 1974.

3*C*: *A Third Collection*. Ed. Frederick E. Crowe, New York: Paulist Press, 1985.

CWL, 1: *Collected Works of Bernard Lonergan*. Vol. 1, [*Grace and Freedom: Operative Grace in the Thought of St. Thomas Aquinas*] Ed. Frederick E. Crowe and Robert M. Doran, Toronto: University of Toronto Press, 2000.

CWL, 2: *Collected Works of Bernard Lonergan*. Vol. 2, [*Verbum: Word and Idea in Aquinas*] Ed. Frederick E. Crowe and Robert M. Doran, Toronto: University of Toronto Press, 1997.

CWL, 3: *Collected Works of Bernard Lonergan*. Vol. 3, [*Insight*] Ed. Frederick E. Crowe and Robert M. Doran, Toronto: University of Toronto Press, 1992.

CWL, 4: *Collected Works of Bernard Lonergan*. Vol. 4, [*Collection*] Ed. Frederick E. Crowe and Robert M. Doran, Toronto: University of Toronto Press, 1988.

CWL, 6: *Collected Works of Bernard Lonergan*. Vol. 6, [*Philosophical and Theological Papers 1958-1964*] Ed. Robert C. Croken, Frederick E. Crowe, and Robert M. Doran, Toronto: University of Toronto Press, 1996.

CWL, 7: *Collected Works of Bernard Lonergan*. Vol. 7, [*The Ontological and Psychological Constitution of Christ*] Ed. Frederick E. Crowe and Robert M. Doran, Tr. M. Shields, Toronto: University of Toronto Press, 2002.

CWL, 17: *Collected Works of Bernard Lonergan*. Vol. 17, [*Philosophical and Theological Papers 1965-1980*] Ed. Robert C. Croken and Robert M. Doran, Toronto: University of Toronto Press, 2004.

Karl Rahner

SW: Spirit in the World. Tr. William Dych, New York: Herder and Herder, 1968, 2nd ed., New York: Continuum, 1994.

HW: Hearer of the Word. Tr. Joseph Donceel, New York: Continuum, 1994. *Hearer* exists in two German editions, the original 1941 edition and a second modified edition edited by Johann Baptist Metz in 1963. For the first edition in English, see *Hearer of the Word*, Tr. Joseph Donceel, New

York: Continuum, 1994; for the second edition, see *Hearers of the Word*, Tr. M. Richards, (New York: Herder), 1969.

TI: *Theological Investigations*. 23 vols. Various Translators. London: Darton, Longman & Todd, 1961-1984.

FCF: *Foundations of Christian Faith: An Introduction to the Idea of Christianity*. Tr. William Dych, London: Darton, Longman & Todd, 1978.

LThK: *Lexikon für Theologie und Kirche*. 10 vols. Ed. Karl Rahner & Josef Höfer. Freiburg: Herder, 2nd ed., 1957-65.

SM: *Sacramentum Mundi*. *An Encyclopedia of Theology*. 6 vols. Ed. Karl Rahner & Adolf Darlap et al. New York: Herder and Herder, 1968-70.

SaW: *Karl-Rahner: Sämtliche Werke*. Ed. Karl Lehmann, Johann Baptist Metz, Karl-Heinz Neufeld, Albert Raffelt and Herbert Vorgrimler. Freiburg: Herder, 1995ff.

Introduction: Celebrating Rahner and Lonergan*

—— Declan Marmion ——
& Raymond Moloney

The year 2004 marks the centenary of the births of two of the outstanding theologians of the twentieth century – the Jesuits Karl Rahner, SJ and Bernard Lonergan, SJ. Each influenced in his own way generations of theologians and philosophers and continues to be discussed today.

Approaching Rahner

Karl Rahner was born in 1904 in Freiburg, Germany. After leaving school he joined the Society of Jesus and was ordained in 1932. Though initially destined for a philosophical career, his dissertation, a study of the epistemology of Thomas Aquinas in the light of modern philosophy (Rahner had attended the seminars of Martin Heidegger in Freiburg) was rejected by his rather traditional supervisor. Though later published as *Spirit in the World*, Rahner would move on a more explicitly theological path – spanning almost half a century – writing on a bewildering variety of topics including spirituality, anthropology, theological

* A version of this introduction first appeared in *The Furrow* 55 (2004): pp. 483-90.

methodology, ecclesiology, Christology and religious pluralism.

His literary output was prodigious – even by 1974 it had reached almost 3000 publications. He preferred to stress the *ad hoc* nature of his writings describing himself as a dilettante. Many of the articles in *Theological Investigations* were originally talks prepared for particular occasions. Rahner never claimed to offer a fully developed systematic theology along the lines of Karl Barth, for example. Nevertheless, for the student approaching his work it can be a daunting task to know exactly where to start.

One approach is to begin with a series of interviews he gave over twenty years, collated as *Karl Rahner in Dialogue: Conversations and Interviews 1965-1982*, translated by Harvey Egan, (1986). This is a fine overview of many of the main themes of Rahner's theology in an engaging style, and Rahner's passion and personality emerge in a way that is not always the case in his *Theological Investigations*.

A Union of the Spiritual and the Theological

Rahner resists easy categorisation. Though traditionally classified as a transcendental Thomist, there are consistent spiritual, ecclesial and pastoral threads underlying his work. His early writings included the bestselling book of prayers *Encounters with Silence* (1938), a work on the history and practice of spirituality with Marcel Viller, and collaboration with his brother Hugo on Ignatian spirituality. Indeed, Rahner was later to claim that it was Ignatius of Loyola who had the most significant influence on his work and that he had tried to incorporate some of the 'existentialism' of Ignatius into his theology. He frequently gave retreats and conferences on Ignatius' *Spiritual Exercises*, the aim of which, according to Rahner, is to facilitate a personal experience of

God so as to discern what God is saying to a person in the particular circumstances of his or her life.

A similar dynamic is at work in Rahner's renewal of the theology of grace. Whereas traditional theology had focused on grace as a habit or quality of the soul infused by God, Rahner's stress is on the personal and experiential aspect of, what he described as, God's 'self-communication.' This stress on a personal experience of God, he maintained, was vital if Christianity was to have a future. As societal supports for Christianity recede, the Christian of the future, he once said, will need to to be a mystic, to draw strength from within, to be one who has experienced God and who can communicate that experience to others.

This conviction that theology cannot be divorced from experiential knowledge of God is one of the reasons, I believe, for Rahner's perennial contemporaneity. He did not simply deal with human experience in general, or in the abstract, but explored the depths of his *own* human and Christian experience. This is why he kept insisting, in his later years, that his life and work could not be separated. His 'spiritual' writings were not merely the 'overflow' or practical application of his more scientific, theological or philosophical investigations. In this sense, what Rahner once said of Aquinas can also be said of him:

> Thomas' *theology is his spiritual life and his spiritual life is his theology.* With him we do not yet find the horrible difference which is often to be observed in later theology, between theology and spiritual life. He thinks theology because he needs it in his spiritual life as its most essential condition, and he thinks theology in such a way that it can become really important for life in the concrete.[1]

Reform in the Church

Not that Rahner's work was overly focused on the individual's experience with God. He had been a *peritus* or theological consultant at Vatican II and made frequent pleas for the renewal of structures within the Church. He looked forward to a less euro-centric, more tolerant and lay-centred Church, mandated by the ecclesiology of Vatican II. However, Rahner grew increasingly impatient and gloomy towards the end of his life at what he saw as a growing restorationist tendency particularly in official circles with more and more ecclesial decision-making taking place in Rome.

Rahner never claimed his theology was the last word or that it was unnecessary to move beyond him. He was variously criticised for being either too radical, or not radical enough. Catholic traditionalists complained that he relativised the radical demands of Christianity. Hans Urs von Balthasar, for example, opined that Rahner's anthropologically-oriented theology reduced Christian living to a bland and shallow humanism. The divergences between the two need to be seen against their different backgrounds, temperament and training. Balthasar, the refined aristocrat, was more influenced by the figures of Goethe and Mozart, more at home with the arts than with politics, more phenomenological in his theological approach. If Rahner understands God in terms of the striving of the human spirit and the pre-apprehension of being, Balthasar's approach is more 'from above' stressing that God is first to be praised and served in obedient discipleship. He was convinced that Rahner's theology was too limited by his philosophy with its focus on transcendental ideas and notions.

Rahner and Beyond: His Legacy Today

At the other end of the theological spectrum, political theologian Johann Baptist Metz argued that Rahner did not give sufficient importance to the societal dimension of Christianity. The categories most prominent in his theology, he pointed out, are the categories of the intimate, the private and the apolitical. An out and out transcendental theology runs the risk of not having to enter the field of history since the human person 'is 'always already,' whether he or she wants to be or not, 'with God."

Rahner, for his part, tried to steer a middle course between the privatisation of Christianity, on the one hand, and its reduction to a purely humanitarian commitment on the other. He supported Metz's political theology agreeing that theology must criticise those structures in society that oppress individuals and groups. He increasingly sought to complement his transcendental approach with an incorporation of a more historical perspective – demonstrated in his choice of theological topics.

Yet, in all of this, Rahner did not want to lose sight of the 'always greater' God, the God of 'incomprehensible mystery,' who cannot be grasped with rationalistic clarity. This led him to appeal for a greater modesty in theological discourse. In this, his theology has affinities with some postmodern theological concerns. More radical postmodern stances, of course, eschew all attempts to construct some grand narrative or overarching theoretical system. There is no fixed meaning to anything – whether world, word, text or individual human subject. The centre does not hold because there is no centre. A more moderate form of postmodernism, however, while resisting the search for the means to ground knowledge in a context-neutral fashion, which it regards as illusory, recognises truth only relative to the community in which a person participates. It is this latter approach which has affinities with Rahner's *Denkstil*, one which does not succumb to total epistemological scepticism, and one which has helped theology come to terms with the situated, partial and fragile character of all human knowing and doing.

By taking seriously the pluralistic, contextual and interdisciplinary nature of theology, Rahner anticipated many of the themes that preoccupy the current postmodern theological scene. Religious scholars, influenced by the writings of Derrida, Levinas, Marion and others, insist that our language about God is inadequate if not idolatrous. In reviving the apophatic tradition, they too, not unlike Rahner before them, are advocating a new, more tentative, way of speaking about God.

Without wishing to turn Rahner into a postmodernist, his theology has at times anticipated some of the characteristics of this style of thinking. In drawing attention to the intellectual pluralism of modern society, he was aware of the inescapability and the irreducible nature of such pluralism and the impossibility of integrating the many different schools of theological thought. In the light of the explosion in scientific knowledge too, the 'abstractness' of his theological concepts became increasingly clear to him. In sum, Rahner's lifelong testimony to the mystery of God as integral to the Christian tradition is probably the greatest achievement of this 'unsystematic' theologian.

Rahner and Lonergan

Bernard Lonergan provides a useful example of a different way of doing theology, while remaining within the same context of the Catholic dogmatic tradition. Born in the same year as Rahner, they both entered the Society of Jesus in their eighteenth year. At that time there was a largely uniform pattern of training in the order, so that the education of both scholars would have many similarities, nourished along the way by the same spirituality.

Lonergan combined his studies of philosophy in Heythrop College, Oxfordshire, with a BA in languages and mathematics at the University of London. His interest in mathematics and science was a life-long one, and eventually had a definite influence in his notion of theological method. He studied theology in Rome in the years leading up to the Second World War, completing his doctorate in 1940. After some intervening years teaching theology in his own country, he returned to Rome to lecture there on dogmatic theology, especially in Christology and Trinity, from 1953 to 1965.

The huge lecture-hall of the Gregorian University brought before him in a very immediate way the problem posed by a diversity of philosophies, even among the disciplined ranks of Catholic seminarians. It also raised the concerns that would lead eventually to his work on theological method. In particular he began to reflect in a sustained way on the different kinds of understanding involved in the various disciplines, in literature, in science, and in the various departments of theology. These were the problems with which he grappled in his monumental philosophical work, *Insight: A Study of Human Understanding*, first published in 1957. As a teacher of theology Lonergan was concerned about the philosophical underpinning of the faith and about how to find some basis on which a reasonable consensus might be sought, to guide us through what he called the 'polymorphism' of contemporary thought.

A 'Rational' Theologian

One of the key principles of Lonergan's approach rests on the fact that all human beings have minds, and our minds function according to a readily recognisable pattern. Lonergan felt that this pattern could become a basis for some unity in our approach to the diversity of fields and systems with which we are confronted. From this emerges his famous four-fold pattern of human thinking: experiencing, understanding, judging and deciding. This aspect of his teaching has been found very helpful in philosophical circles and, for students in particular, forms a gateway into many of the problems before them.

Not so easy to grasp is the underlying principle of this structure, especially that which concerns the difference between the second and the third stages in this pattern. This is a structure for reaching the real, and Lonergan has a certain view of what realism means. He calls it a critical realism, which he distinguishes clearly from another interpretation which he calls an immediate realism. The distinction between these two, as he interprets them, is one of the basic discoveries of his system of thought, and he tells us in the Introduction to *Insight* that 'one has not made it yet if one has no clear memory of its startling strangeness.' Lonergan considers that this discovery, which in a later work he calls intellectual conversion, is comparatively rare on the academic plane. Consequently he finds himself ploughing a somewhat different furrow to that of many of his philosophical and theological colleagues.

Method in Theology
In the middle of the 1960's illness put an end to Lonergan's tenure in the Gregorian University. He returned to his own country and after a few years was able to resume his academic studies in Regis College, Toronto. These studies bore fruit in 1972 with the publication of his second major work, *Method in Theology*, a programmatical essay on the nature of theology in the light of a contemporary philosophy. Lonergan continued contributing to conferences and learned publications for the rest of his career, taking part in the annual workshops on his

writings in Boston College. During these years he received considerable international recognition, being honoured with no less than 19 honorary degrees from universities in Canada and the United States. He received one of his country's highest civil awards, being made a Companion of the Order of Canada in 1971, and a Fellow of the British Academy in 1975.

Lonergan's contribution to theology is somewhat different from that of his German confrère. The works that reflect the earlier part of his career, when he was lecturing in Rome, are significant, first of all, in the historical dimension they add to the study of Christology and of the Trinity. In his treatises on these subjects, his view in the former of the consciousness of Christ, and his view in the latter of the Trinity as a community of conscious subjects, represent high-points of theological insight, which the reflection of subsequent theologians has scarcely done justice to.

However, as regards the actual treatment of concrete theological issues, it must be pointed out that his publications, while valuable in themselves, are nowhere as wide-ranging or as immediate as those of Karl Rahner. When Lonergan returned to his task after his illness, he operated under a certain 'self-denying ordinance', electing to leave to others the many concrete issues of the day in order to concentrate on the one concern which he felt was crucial for all the rest and yet neglected by most, namely the question of method. His study *Insight* was a remote preparation for treating this latter question. The issue was a recurrent theme in his publications in the intervening years; and then came his crowning work, *Method in Theology*.

Only in this book do we meet the mature Lonergan. Readers of *Insight* have sometimes felt out of sympathy with the rigorous intellectualism of that earlier work. In *Method in*

Theology Lonergan advances to a more holistic treatment of the human subject, where the volitional and affective aspects of the person are better integrated into the total picture. This enables him to face up to some of the crucial hermeneutical problems that have dogged theology, especially since the time of Heidegger and Bultmann. Drawing also on some key concepts of spirituality, he is able to give an account not only of the nature of theology itself, but of the kind of person a theologian must be. No longer is theology to be described as the science of God. A basis has now been worked out on which theology can be satisfactorily distinguished from religion, and theology is seen as reflection on religion, and its role is to mediate between religion and culture. As for the theologian, he or she must be a person intellectually, morally and religiously converted, for, as Augustine said, in a phrase beloved by Heidegger, only through love does one enter into truth.

Lonergan's key contribution, then, is to be characterised more on the level of performance than of content. He made a deliberate choice to concentrate on understanding what is involved in the actual process of doing theology rather than on wrestling with particular theological issues in themselves. It was a choice for quality rather than for quantity, for depth rather than for range. While his work therefore might seem restricted in respect of the number of topics discussed, its potential relevance is as wide as the entire field of theology.

Method in Theology is the watershed from which there has come a flood-tide of subsequent reflection and publication, as scholars in various countries labour at the immense task of implementing the programme Lonergan has outlined, and at applying his principles in various concrete issues. The disciplines in which his approach is found relevant include not only the various branches of theology but also philosophy, literature, jurisprudence and even economics. A scholar from Uppsala some time ago maintained that the number of theses world-wide on Lonergan exceeds even the number on Rahner!

Lonergan's study of method is no straightforward book. Even Rahner in his one essay on the topic seems to have missed the point. The criterion for judging Lonergan, therefore, lies not in the number of theological questions which he himself has illuminated in his writings, but in the vitality of the movement engendered by his method, and in the success with which it is found by subsequent scholars to confront the pluralism, polymorphism and chaos of contemporary academic thought.

Why This Book?

The collection of papers in this book is the fruit of an international conference to mark the centenaries of the births of Bernard Lonergan and Karl Rahner hosted by the Milltown Institute of Philosophy and Theology in Dublin in November 2004. The conference explored aspects of the legacies of these two philosopher/theologians by examining not only their respective contributions to philosophy and theology but also by bringing their insights into dialogue with many of the issues facing Christians today. Thus the reader will find themes such as postmodernity, spiritual experience, interreligious dialogue, religious pluralism and mission interwoven in dialogue with the perspectives of Rahner and Lonergan. It is not that the speakers considered Rahner or Lonergan the last word on such topics or agreed with them on all matters. In fact, some of the issues taken up here only appear implicitly in their work. Yet all the contributors see Rahner and Lonergan as important voices – and not only from the past. Rahner, for example, was very much a practical and contextual theologian, while Lonergan's methodological investigations continue to be influential.

In the first part of the book, William Mathews brings Lonergan's anthropological insights into dialogue with recent voices from the worlds of natural science and literature, while Michael McCabe explores the anthropological perspectives of Rahner and their implications for mission. Part two focuses on the renewal of theology since Vatican II and here Cynthia Crysdale develops some overlooked aspects of Lonergan's epistemological legacy from a feminist perspective. Dermot Lane then discusses the importance of interreligious dialogue and analyses Rahner's contribution to the topic. Part three takes up the issue of theology in the university with specific reference to the Irish context. Here Eamonn Conway (and Linda Hogan in her response) explores how theology might find an appropriate place in a rapidly changing university context where the role of the Humanities is often undermined by the ideology of the market. Michael Paul Gallagher and Declan Marmion in part four discuss the question of Christian identity in a postmodern age taking their cue from Lonergan and Rahner respectively. The final part of the book – with contributions from Hilary Mooney, Philip Endean and Raymond Moloney – looks at the notion of religious experience in Rahner and Lonergan in relation to contemporary developments in spirituality. We hope that the varied themes discussed here will serve not only as a tribute to Rahner and Lonergan but also be a contribution to some of the more pressing challenges facing Christians in our postmodern age.

The impetus for the conference came from the President of the Institute, Brian Grogan, SJ. Thanks are due to him for his support and encouragement and also to the organising committee: Declan Marmion, SM, William Mathews, SJ, and

Raymond Moloney, SJ. Irene Hickey provided invaluable marketing, catering and other assistance. Gesa Thiessen, the staff at the Registry in Milltown Institute, and the administration at Milltown Park were also most helpful. The Irish and Canadian Province of the Society of Jesus contributed significant financial sponsorship. The Archbishop of Dublin, Diarmuid Martin graciously officiated at the opening of the conference. Various colleagues chaired and facilitated the different sessions. Thomas Dalzell and Gesa Thiessen proof-read portions of the text. Helen Carr and Daragh Reddin at Veritas Publications facilitated the publishing of the papers and provided much needed help and encouragement at various stages of production. To all the above, and to all who took part in the conference, our sincere thanks.

Notes
1 'Thomas Aquinas,' *Everyday Faith*, London: Burns and Oates, 1967, p. 188.

I.

The Mystery of the Human

CHAPTER ONE

The Mystery of the Human: A Perspective from Lonergan

—— William Mathews ——

After a survey of some anthropological challenges from science, literature and history the present chapter turns to the anthropologies of Lonergan's *Insight* and *Method in Theology*. It concludes with some reflections on the significance of his notion of human historicity.

1. The Human Mystery in the Life Sciences

In an interview published in the *New York Times* on 13 April 2004, shortly before he died of cancer, Francis Crick, the celebrated co-discoverer of DNA made some highly revealing remarks. He was obsessed, he admitted, from very early on in his career by two problems, 'the borderline between the living and the non-living and the nature of consciousness.' It is a strong statement about the intellectual desires which motivated him and which, in their own way, gave his life its particular shape, its intellectual identity. He wanted to get to the bottom of these mysteries and, in his later years, did not welcome invitations for public appearances as they interrupted his train of thought.

With James Watson in 1953 he discovered that the chemical DNA was basic to all organic life. It seems to have been his conclusion, as was that of Watson, that DNA contained, so to speak, the secret of life. Since its discovery life was now reduced to chemistry. When Crick moved on to the problem of explaining consciousness something of the same mind-set remained. As the secret of organic life was hidden in DNA, so the secret of consciousness, the human mystery is hidden in a sub-set of the neural structures of the brain. When we have discovered them, the DNA so to speak, of consciousness, we will have unveiled its secret. My own view is that the life principles in the living cell manipulate the DNA rather than the opposite as insights manipulate images and cannot be reduced to them.

The quest to unpack the secret of consciousness became Crick's passion. Involved in it was his peculiarly reductionist anthropology, reductionism being, as Edward Wilson's book, *Consilience*, makes clear, the religious faith of very many scientists.[1] In that spirit Crick, in his book, *The Astonishing Hypothesis: The Scientific Search for the Soul* wrote:

> Your joys and sorrows, your memories and your ambitions, your sense of personal identity and free will, are in fact no more than the behaviour of a vast assembly of nerve cells and their associated molecules.[2]

Against the belief of Colin McGinn and Stephen Pinker, who maintain that an ultimate explanation of consciousness will elude us, Crick believes that it is within our reach. When reached it will result in the death of the soul, at which point educated people will believe there is no soul independent of the body, no life after death.

What is clear from this is that Francis Crick, for all his brilliance, and I highly respect that, has never read Aristotle's *Peri Psyches*, that is to say, on the psyche or soul. For Aristotle the soul is the life principle of the body – organic, sensory and intellectual. It is also, in its intellectual dimension of the agent intellect, the principle of all intellectual inquiry in the empirical sciences. Francis Crick is a wonderful example of the activity of what Aristotle means by the intellectual soul arguing that it does not exist. He has no interest in getting to the bottom of the desires in himself that motivate his quest to master DNA and the neural basis of consciousness.

Despite this, geneticists and the life scientists have made an outstanding contribution to the extremely thorny problem of demolishing the colonial notion of race. Stemming from the coloniser's view of their conquests there arose the notion of a hierarchy of races, from the less primitive and ignorant to the more advanced and intelligent. This disturbing attitude to human differences reached its high point as recently as the early 1940s in the master race theory of the Third Reich. In 1996 in their work *African Exodus: The Origins of Modern Humanity*, Chris Stringer and Robin McKie began to make available to a wider public the emerging theory of the African origins of the entire human family.[3] In one fell swoop the earlier theories of a master and subordinate races were destroyed. Biologically, we are all parts of one and the same tree of life. This has been further developed in Stephen Oppenheimer's *Out of Eden* which, on the basis of genetics and culture, has established that the entire world outside of Africa was populated by a migration of an African population of some 250 individuals across the sea to the Yemen around 80,000 years ago.[4]

There is involved in this one of the most fascinating paradigm shifts of our time, but there is a sting in the tail concerning the problem of the defining features of the human being. Many of the modern anthropologists who address the question about human origins tend towards the view that what we think of as defining human features; language, culture and the human form of consciousness are largely biological refinements of our animal predecessors.

2. Walker Percy and Literature

Turning next to literature, I single out from many possible sources the searching of Walker Percy, brought to my attention by Paul Elie's engaging *The Life You Save May Be Your Own, An American Pilgrimage.*[5] Percy was educated in the sciences as part of his training as a doctor but contracted TB and during his rehabilitation read the works of Camus, Sartre and especially Kierkegaard. As a result he became a writer, married and became a Catholic. Why did he become a Catholic? Because, according to Carl Olson, of the anthropological problem:

> Percy rightly dismissed the notion that people can live without an anthropological vision, that is, a specific understanding of who man is and what he is meant for. 'Everyone has an anthropology,' he wrote in the essay, 'Rediscovering a Canticle for Leibowitz.' 'There is no not having one. If a man says he does not, all he is saying is that his anthropology is implicit, a set of assumptions which he has not thought to call into question.' His own conversion was due, in large part, to the realization that scientism – the belief that the scientific method and the technology it produces can provide answers to man's deepest questions and longings – was untenable and, in fact, was a lie.[6]

To which Percy added:

> This life is much too much trouble, far too strange, to arrive at the end of it and then be asked what you make

of it and have to answer: scientific humanism. That won't do. A poor show. Life is a mystery, love is a delight. Therefore, I take it as axiomatic that one should settle for nothing less than the infinite mystery and the infinite delight, God. [7]

According to Elie, when Percy made the transition from being a doctor who believed in the world view of the sciences to an author whose task was to diagnose the human condition, he needed some measure of the human to aid him on his task.

This is what he claimed he found in Catholicism, and specifically in what he called Christian anthropology. Catholicism, as he put it, considers the human person part angel, part beast. It locates *the* divided human nature at the center of its scheme and asks the right questions: Why are so many of us unhappy? Why is there such cruelty in the world? It also gives a powerfully suggestive answer: The human person – as Percy understood it – is a creature suspended between two infinities, a pilgrim and wayfarer. We don't know quite where we came from or where we are going. Man is born to trouble 'as the sparks fly up.'[8]

His breakthrough in his quest came in the sanatorium when he read Kierkegaard's famous passage 'describing Hegel as the philosopher who lived in a shanty outside the palace of his own system and saying that Hegel knew everything and said everything, except what it was to be born and to live and to die.'[9] Hegel left out the one thing worth knowing, the significance of the individual life. Many modern thinkers have settled everything 'except what it is to live as an individual. He still has to get through an ordinary Wednesday afternoon ... What does this man do with the rest of the day? The rest of his life?'[10] The challenge here is to try and understand how we ought to live our individuality, our unique providentially ordained selfhood. Any contemporary anthropology has to acknowledge that the sheer range of the extremes that we find in individual human lives are perplexing, from a hospice nurse to a hostage taker or murderer, from a psychopath to a saint. In short, every individual is their own distinct solution to the problem of living but those solutions are not worked out in solitary isolation from others. In *The Human Condition* Hannah Arendt makes clear that it is through the interaction of diversities of human forms of life that individual life stories emerge.[11] Our twenty-first century anthropological landscape and context, moreover, are framed and shaped by a sense of fragmentation, of childhood from old age, public life from private. This emphasis on parts leaves us with no sense of the unity that we are or of the social world to which we belong.[12] The complexity of our own lives and world is largely beyond our comprehension.

As well as the great human creativity illustrated in twentieth century science and technology, literature and art, historical studies such as those of Anthony Beevor's three books on *Stalingrad*, *Berlin* and the *The Spanish Civil War* must also come into the anthropological equation.[13] Daniel Levinson in his discussion of mid-life in his *Seasons of a Man's Life* draws our attention to the polarity of creativity and destructiveness.[14] Beevor's books are epics of human destructiveness. The sheer dehumanisation of ordinary Russian and German folk in the course of those wars, the depths of depravity which emerged from them, more than astonish. They point to the fundamental anthropological thesis of Hannah Arendt that in totalitarian regimes there is a culture of death and individual lives are worthless. Such possibilities, it seems, are always latent in the human community. A contemporary anthropology can thus have no illusions any more. Anthropologists must struggle to become open to the full range of the human condition as presented in the totality of their world culture and history and the questions it brings to them.

3. The Anthropology of Insight

Every human work, a book or an artefact, even a form of life has both its cultural and anthropological presuppositions and significance. These may be direct or indirect. The author may in fact express or comment directly on their view of the human being and related human condition, as in Picasso's *Guernica* or in Walker Percy's *The Moviegoer*. More indirectly the works may reveal to us something about the values and disvalues of their authors as human and their related form of life.

From this perspective if one reads the first eight chapters of *Insight* one will quickly see a division there between an engagement, on the one hand, with the very technical disciplines of mathematics and the empirical sciences, and on the other, with the very dramatic and intersubjective realm of common sense and its world of community and history. *Insight* presupposes that we are all members, in our own ways, of such relatively advanced communities with their horizons or worlds. What it is attempting to do is to make sense of that fact, to understand the implicit mind-world relations that are involved.

The Scientific Community and World – the Desire of the Mind
The mathematical and scientific forms of life are, for Lonergan, the example, par excellence of the human desire to understand, explain, make sense of and master, and, in those pursuits of the experience of the intellectual pattern of experience:

Deep within us all, emergent when the noise of other appetites is stilled, there is a drive to know, to understand, to see why, to discover the reason, to find the cause, to explain. Just what is wanted, has many names. In precisely what it consists, is a matter of dispute. But the fact of inquiry is beyond all doubt. It can absorb a man.[15]

In this context we can think of the intellectual passion to understand of an Archimedes, Galileo, Newton, Darwin, Einstein, Freud, Crick and Chomsky. Anthropologically, Lonergan is interested in what it is that is in us all in different degrees that gives rise to these lives. He also makes it clear that it is one thing to be characterised by an unusual desire to understand some feature of one's world, it is another thing to understand that mental performance. What exactly do we mean by the eros of the mind? What is it like and what is it for?

In response Lonergan offers the reader a series of intellectual exercises whose goal is to enable them to develop a heightened awareness of their potential intellectual curiosity and the manner in which it structures their knowing on the levels of the senses and imagination, understanding and conceptualisation, and finally of judgment. Usually students develop a familiarity with the language of desire or puzzlement and insight, and feel they have some form of mastery of the problem of consciousness. Unfortunately, as is frequently the case, language can conceal much more than it reveals, and thus can conceal what it ought to be disclosing, namely, the startling strangeness of the mental. Let me see if I can shock you into appreciating that startling strangeness.

In the preface to *Insight* Lonergan remarks that it is his goal to work out a philosophy based on an insight into insight, compare it with one based on insight into oversights, and so get to the roots of the problem of progress and decline. This might sound plausible but it poses fascinating and disturbing questions about the nature of consciousness. The problem is that, for Aquinas, insights are into phantasms, that is to say, imaginative presentations or data, this being the case even for our knowledge of God. It is also the case that what they grasp is not the presentations as sensible but what they represent, these being beyond the capabilities of our senses and imagination. But our desire to understand and the insights it seeks in response as conscious activities of the cognitional subject are a real but unimaginable conscious awareness. Because the desire that moves and the event of insight cannot be imagined, neither can they be directly represented in an image or phantasm. If this is the case, there can be no insights directly into insights or into any other conscious aspects of human cognition such as judgment. If we are to understand intellectual desire as conscious it will not be directly, through some form of inner intellectual look. It will come about indirectly through the medium of an appropriate language which articulates the details of the problem-solving performance as a whole, the matter, so to speak, of which the desire and related insights are the form.

The Common Sense Community and World – the Conflict of Consciousness.

If the chapters on science presuppose the intellectual world, with its emphasis on mathematics and science, in which Lonergan was educated, those on common sense presuppose the historical world in which he lived and experienced, especially during his Rome years in the 1930s. The same intellectual capacities that operate in science also operate in the life of the subject and worlds of common sense. But there is a difference. Whereas in science the human animal, so to speak, has to recede, in common sense it can be a dominant factor. Lonergan uses the terms 'polymorphism' and 'dialectic' to discuss this core tension within human consciousness: 'the tension between incompletely developed intelligence and imperfectly adapted sensibility grounds the dialectics of individual and social history.'[16]

What exactly he means by our human sensibility, human intersubjectivity, human spontaneity and intersubjective spontaneity, is problematic. Simone de Beauvoir deals with essentially the same problem in her *Ethics of Ambiguity* in terms of the language of ambiguity. Referring back to the Athenian myth of human origins as in the earth rather than in the gods, she continues that there is a fundamental ambiguity to human life. Every human exists at the same time in two realms: 'he is still part of the world of which he is a consciousness.'[17] Rooted as they are in the earth, humans can transcend their material origin in thought, but they can never escape it. For de Beauvoir, the ambiguity of the human condition is, as for Kierkegaard, tragic.

Materialist philosophers reduce one side of this pair, mind, to the other, matter or embodiment; idealists do the opposite. Dualists settle for a permanent standoff in which both co-exist in the individual human being, in Francois Jeanson's words, 'like eternal strangers.'[18] For de Beauvoir, following Hegel on master and slave, the ambiguity of human existence has profound implications for the way we relate to others, for there is in our earthy nature an instinctive and spontaneous will to power, a desire to dominate the other and to establish sovereignty.

For Lonergan the tension between incompletely developed intelligence and imperfectly adapted sensibility expresses itself in the biases of common sense, dramatic, individual, group and general. In each of these, individually and collectively in the members and leaders of the group or nation, our spontaneous sensibilities inhibit our freedom to raise and pursue important questions which are significant for the proper conduct of our lives. The biases that result shape the dialectics of individual and social history. What his analysis needs to bring out much more forcefully is the harm which those biases cause in the interpersonal domain. By dramatic bias is meant all those realms of our own personal experiences in the daily drama of our lives in relation to which we are in denial. By individual bias is meant all those realms where we cultivate a philosophy of individualism which always puts us first at the expense of others. By group bias Lonergan is referring to situations when a particular group and its leaders, the patriarchy or a particular powerful ethnic or religious group, puts itself forward in relation to other groups as the dominant group at the centre of the universe. What is involved is not an intellectual game as the suffering caused by the racism that Martin Luther King tried to face down in the US in the '60s or Nelson Mandela in South Africa shows. By general bias Lonergan means the inability of common sense to understand that it cannot think on the level of history and that if it does not understand the limits of its competence then chaos will result. The biases of common sense and their consequences are the product of a core conflict at the heart of the human. In *Insight*, it could be argued, Lonergan does not adequately articulate just how deep the conflict between these two orientations in human consciousness runs and the interpersonal and social violence of its consequences.

4. The Anthropology of Method in Theology

In contrast with the passionate intellectualism of *Insight*, *Method in Theology*, written to help him convalesce from a severe and life-threatening encounter with lung cancer, during which he experienced profound care and love by a nursing sister, reads differently. It presupposes that the theologian is a member of a religious community and culture and that the human community is at every point in its history faced with the challenge of differentiating between progress and decline – 'A civilization in decline digs its own grave with a relentless consistency. It cannot be argued out of its self-destructive ways.'[19] In this context a theology becomes a reflection on the religion of a culture.

Although *Method* lacks the expansiveness of *Insight* and its minimalism needs to be opened up, there is a new emphasis in it on feelings and love: 'Intermediate between judgments of fact and judgments in value lie apprehensions of value; such apprehensions are given in feelings.'[20] That feelings respond to values in accordance with some scale of preferences needs to be acknowledged as well as the fact that there can also be aberrant feelings.

This emphasis on the relation between feelings and values is part of his growing awareness of the greater significance of the ethical. Beginning shortly after *Insight*, by his 1964 essay, 'Existenz and Aggiornamento,' he was stating that the being of the subject is a becoming in which decision making is central. The magnitude of this shift, the enlargement of his vision of the human from a pursuit of being to a pursuit of the worthwhile and the prominence in it of the role of feelings, is quite startling. If the heart of *Insight* could be summed up in terms of an effort to understand our intellectual passion, *Method* could be summed up as an effort to understand our ethical passion. That passion, deep within us, emerges when the noise of other appetites is stilled as a drive to find something worthwhile to do in the world and, in creatively building up that good, to become someone worthwhile. That project for him can never be achieved in isolation and so in section 6 of chapter two on 'The Human Good' in *Method in Theology*, a sketch is offered of the meshing of the individual and the social processes. But again the analysis is minimal and needs to be expanded.

Religion

As the pursuit of the human good of order is a social collaboration, so Lonergan has remarked that religion is both personal and a social good of order. And it is on the religious level that his philosophy of the self further expands into the interpersonal:

> ... [B]eyond the moral operator that promotes us from judgments of facts to judgments of value with their retinue of decisions and actions, there is a further realm of interpersonal relations and total commitment in which human beings tend to find the immanent goal of their being and, with it, their fullest joy and deepest peace.[21]

The potential latent in our core desires for truth and value, what Lonergan names the transcendental notions, becomes self-transcending, an achievement when one falls in love. As human love leads to a sharing of knowledge not otherwise accessible, so faith is the knowledge that is born of religious love. 'In the light of faith, originating value is the divine light and love, while terminal value is the whole universe ... Without faith, without the eye of love, the world is too evil for God to be good, for a good God to exist.'[22] This, in turn, enables us to cope with the betrayals, humiliations and failures in life. When that sense of being loved is absent life becomes trivialised and harsh, power ruthlessly exercised, and existence absurd.[23]

Genuine religion is discovered and realised by redemption from the many traps of religious aberration. Religious development goes beyond the opposition between contrary propositions to engage directly with real and conflicting oppositions within the human family of individuals and groups. In this a religion is clearly distinct from its theology. Its educator is not just some *a priori* construction of categories but also the discerning study of human history. It follows that the love of God that religion calls forth is anything but an opium of the people. It does not directly eliminate the conflicts within consciousness already noted but makes them bearable. Personal and social religious development entails a constant struggle with a core conflict at the heart of religious consciousness between the polarities of true and false love. All of this points to the need for a theological anthropology that is rooted in the study of history and in the concrete details of the problem of the self and the other such as we find in Levinas and Simone de Beauvoir.

In a striking passage in the foreword to his *The Way to Nicea* Lonergan acknowledges that there is both live and dead religion. The creativity of a religion can be discerned in its emergence, in its vital acceptance, in living it day by day, in bringing about the adjustments to cultural variation and changing circumstances that the very vitality of a religion demands. So it is, as Wilfred Cantwell Smith remarked, that 'All religions are new religions, every morning. For religions do not exist in the sky somewhere elaborated, finished, and static; they exist in men's hearts.'[24] Lonergan's various remarks on religion suggest the need for a book on that topic which, unfortunately, he never wrote.

5. Historicity and the Human Mystery

After *Method in Theology,* in his 1977 essay 'Natural Right and Historical Mindedness,' the theme of historicity is addressed by Lonergan, a notion of immense anthropological significance:

> A contemporary ontology would distinguish two components in concrete human reality: on the one hand, a constant, human nature; on the other hand a variable, human historicity. Nature is given to man at birth. Historicity is what man makes of man.[25]

In that essay Lonergan gestures towards the richness and complexity of the notion: 'To understand the constant, nature, one may study any individual. But to understand the variable, historicity, one has to study each instance in its singularity.'[26] The implication is that from the perspective of historicity every human being is uniquely distinct, every becoming self is singular, a unique creation which cannot be replaced by or substituted for by someone else. Human beings are not a dime a dozen. There is involved in the addition of historicity to nature an enormous expansion of anthropological horizons that impacts on all the previous points.

For Lonergan the structure or nature of our desire to know and act in the world expresses the conditions of being an authentic person. It is a matter of being attentive, intelligent, reasonable and responsible. But he adds a further precept: 'Moreover, since the actuation of the structure arises under social conditions and within cultural traditions, to the four there may be added a fifth, acknowledge your historicity.'[27] There is a recognition here that, like Hegel, one can assimilate the nature of one's cognitional and ethical structure but that does not help one directly to live one's own particular life with its specific problem solving challenges. Appropriating the historicity of one's desires is a matter of understanding the problems which one's society and culture call on one to engage with, not in the abstract, but concretely. Different chapters in one's intellectual and ethical history will throw up the different problems which, together, make up the storyline, the form or soul of our embodied historicity.

This in turn poses questions such as: how well can we understand the historicity of our own desires or of the desires of another person? Francis Crick did not seem to understand his very well. How well can the desire, and related form of life which authored *Insight*, be understood? These are challenges concretely faced by autobiographers and biographers, the masters of human historicity.

My response to this challenge was helped by a quote by the movie director, Ingmar Bergman about his experience of writing his autobiography. Bergman was the author and producer of such movies as: *The Seventh Seal* (1956), *Wild Strawberries*, (1957), *Through a Glass Darkly* (1960), *Persona* (1965), and *Cries and Whispers* (1971). When he came to reflect on his life in order to write his autobiography he remarked:

> Watching forty years of my work over the span of one year turned out to be unexpectedly upsetting, at times unbearable. I suddenly realized that my movies had mostly been conceived in the depths of my soul, in my heart, my brain, my nerves, my sex, and not least, in my guts. A nameless desire gave them birth. Another desire, which can perhaps be called 'the joy of the craftsman,' brought them that further step where they were displayed to the world.[28]

Bergman acknowledged with puzzlement that all his movies were expressions of some unfathomable desire in him, as well as being explorations of human relations. All creative works in this sense are expressions of some aspect of the desires of their authors, even those of Francis Crick, and in this sense are anthropologically revealing. But it seems to have been Bergman's conclusion that it was impossible to figure out those desires, figure out what they are really like and for, because they were too elusive.

Significant in my quest to understand the historicity of Lonergan's desire was the discovery of the beginnings, the awakenings of his desire as an author to the big questions which he was going to pursue. Between 1926 and 1938 Lonergan's desire to understand was awakened by four distinct problems, the Kantian problem of thought and reality – the mind-world relation; the explanation of the economic cycle; the problem of progress and decline in history; and finally, in 1938, the problem of method in theology. What is significant is that the awakening of his desire is not something that happens inside his solitary consciousness, so to speak. In each case the potential to wonder is awakened and called forth by circumstances and events in the world, a philosophy course, the economic depression, the collapse of European history, and his doctoral dissertation on grace and freedom.

Awakenings are followed by journeying in which in their own erratic way the questions grow and call forth insights. One enters this process by posing questions such as – how did his philosophy courses and teachers influence him? What mark did the books he read leave on his quest? What people were influential in shaping the structure and direction of his questioning? What good luck and bad luck did he endure? What moments of insight did he enjoy? Significant in that process are the moments of decision to author a particular text. In 1943 Lonergan decided to author the *Verbum* articles, in 1945 *Insight*, in 1958 *Method in Theology*. In those decisions are revealed his core values as an author.

Authoring here refers to a time when, although one might not yet have all the necessary insights, the shape of the problems involved has reached maturity. So it was with *Insight*. When he started writing the problems had a certain shape out of which the book grew. In the course of writing he had a whole series of insights into the problem of thought and reality, into cognitional structure, the principal notion of objectivity, emergent probability, the dialectical structure of the development of common sense. Between 1951 and 1953 the process of authoring *Insight* was explosive, titanic. After 1965 when authoring *Method in Theology*, the mood of the process was that of a convalescent.

Engaging with these elements challenges us to comprehend the 28 year journey of the desire of the author that began at Heythrop in 1926 and ended with the completion of *Insight* in 1954 and its publication in 1957. We can of course follow the public face of the desire, of the vision quest with its beginning, journeying and its chapters, time to decide and the time to compose, a public face that also has its expression in conversations, letters, texts, etc.

If the public face of the desire to know is called forth by problems in the world, it is also the case that that face is but one of the two inseparable dimensions of the core desire of the author. As it engages with problems and situations in its world it is at the same time accompanied by an inseparable conscious self-awareness of being in the tension of inquiry which, in a sense, is private. Only when that tension is stilled by the final text, despite its limitations or even imperfections, is the authoring process complete. That conscious tension which always accompanies the engagement of the desires and related journeys of Lonergan, Bergman, Crick, of you and me, concretely with problems and situations in the world can never be severed from its public expression. A great deal of twentieth century thought has tried to eliminate the way in which the desires of an author relate to his or her texts from the process of interpretation. To lose sight of the self-consciousness of the author as the producer of the text is to distort or empty the human being of its core meaning.

My conclusion was that the more I tried to master that desire in its conscious dimension, attempted to reduce it to the level of the familiar, even tame it, the stranger and more mysterious but also, paradoxically, the more real it became. Human consciousness is constituted by a desire structure that is always moving beyond its present achievement, is never satisfied, and as conscious is strangely unimaginable, even irreducibly mysterious. Lonergan, I believe, does not adequately underline this fact.

At the heart of the human journeys of Lonergan, Bergman, Francis Crick, of you and me, is a startlingly strange and mysterious emergent desire, an unimaginable, given, conscious self-awareness. Impossible to read in the early stages or even for most of our lives, though, in some instances with recollection in one's mature years, its strange presence and shape can be faintly detected as emerging and shaping one's historicity. Eventually, to pose the question, 'What are those emergent desires in you like and for?' is, in the company of Walker Percy but not Francis Crick, to have found and addressed your mystery.

Notes

1   Edward Wilson, *Consilience: The Unity of Knowledge*, London: Abacus 1999, p. 58.

2   Francis Crick, *The Astonishing Hypothesis*, London: Simon and Schuster, 1994, p. 3.

3   Chris Stringer and Robin McKie, *African Exodus: The Origins of Modern Humanity*, London: Pimlico, 1996.

4   Stephen Oppenheimer, *Out of Eden, The Peopling of the World*, London: Robinson, 2004.

5   Paul Elie, *The Life You Save May Be Your Own, An American Pilgrimage*, New York: Farrer, Strauss and Giroux, 2003.

6   Carl E. Olson, 'Travelling with Walker Percy,' *Saint Austin Review* 2003, taken from: http://carl-olson.com/articles/wpercy_star.html.

7   *Ibid.*, pp. 2-3.

8   Elie, op. cit., p. 160.

9   *Ibid.*, p. 142.

10   Olson, op cit., p. 3.

11   Hannah Arendt, *The Human Condition*, Chicago: University of Chicago Press, 1958, pp. 175f.

12   Alasdair MacIntyre, *After Virtue, A Study in Moral Theory*, London: Duckworth, 1985, p. 204.

13   Anthony Beevor, *The Spanish Civil War*, London: Cassell, 1999; *Stalingrad*, London: Penguin Books, 1999; *Berlin, the Downfall*, London: Penguin Books, 2003.

14   Daniel Levinson, *The Seasons of a Man's Life*, New York: Ballantine, 1978.

15   *CWL*, 3 [*Insight*], pp. 28-9.

16   *Ibid.*, p. 291.

17   See Kristina Arp, *The Bonds of Freedom, Simone de Beauvoir's Existentialist Ethics*, Chicago: Open Court, 2001, p. 48.

18   Francis Jeanson, *Sartre and the Problem of Morality*, Bloomington: Indiana University Press, 1980, p. 15.

19   *Method*, p. 55.

20   *Ibid.*, p. 37, also p. 31 and p. 33.

21   *CWL*, 17 [*Philosophical and Theological Papers 1965-1980*], p. 400.

22   *Method*, pp. 105, 115-116.

23   *Ibid.*, p. 105.

24   *The Way to Nicea*, London: Darton, Longman and Todd, 1976, p. vii.

25   3*C*, p. 170.

26   *Ibid.*, p. 171.

27   *CWL*, 17, p. 378.

28   Ingmar Bergmann, *Images, My Life in Film*, London: Bloomsbury, 1994. The remark features on the back of the dustcover.

CHAPTER TWO

The Mystery of the Human: A Perspective from Rahner

—— Michael McCabe ——

Introduction

I wish to begin my presentation by honestly admitting that I am no expert on the theology of Karl Rahner, but simply a reflective missionary who, as a student of theology in the immediate aftermath of Vatican II, came under the influence of his theological investigations, and who was and still is greatly impressed by the profundity of his thought and its relevance to the mission of the Church in today's world. Much of Karl Rahner's thought can be viewed as an extended reflection on Augustine's famous dictum: 'Thou hast made us for thyself, O Lord, and our hearts are restless until they find their rest in thee.' The mystery at the heart of human existence is the foundation and constant point of reference in his voluminous writings, grounding Catholic doctrine in human experience, linking spirituality and theology, and opening the Church to the world. Many of Rahner's essays focus explicitly on this theme, which also runs like a silver thread through his extensive corpus of writings, and it would take more than a single paper to explore it adequately. The aim of my presentation is simply to introduce the topic. It is divided into three parts: the first, highlighting Rahner's approach to the presence of mystery in the human experience of self-transcendence; the second, focusing on the mystery of God as the ground and goal of human self-transcendence; third, some implications of Rahner's understanding of the human for understanding the mission of the Church today. Before embarking on this threefold task, let me make a few important preliminary clarifications.

1. Preliminary Clarifications

Rahner's approach to the mystery of the human would seem to have leaned heavily on a philosophical analysis deeply indebted to transcendental Thomism and specifically to the thought of Joseph Maréchal, SJ, (1878-1944). It is fashionable to argue today that, in the later years of his life, Rahner abandoned the philosophical positions he had developed as a young man.[1] According to Philip Endean, however, there is no real evidence for this claim.[2] While Rahner was primarily a theologian, starting from, and informed by, an explicit faith commitment, he was far from averse to using philosophical categories where these helped to illuminate the mysteries of faith for contemporary believers. In Endean's view, it was Rahner's achievement to make a philosophical case for the claim that 'the question about God is at least latent in all human awareness, a question at once unanswerable and inescapable.'[3]

A second preliminary clarification concerns Rahner's understanding of mystery. Rahner emphatically rejected the concept of mystery current in the Catholic manuals of theology that flourished in seminaries from the time of the First Vatican Council to the middle of the last century. These manuals of theology referred to the mysteries of faith as revealed truths which the human mind cannot now understand and which the believer accepts because the

Church teaches them. The implication here is that these truths are mysteries only in a provisional sense and will later on – in heaven – become amenable 'to the demands made by human reason for insight and perspicuousness.'[4] This understanding of mystery, says Rahner, is deficient for several reasons, notably for failing to take account of the religious nature of the revealed Christian mysteries and for failing to show how these mysteries are related to one another to form a coherent whole.[5] For Rahner, 'mystery is not merely a way of saying that reason has not yet completed its victory. It is the goal where reason arrives when it attains its perfection by becoming love.'[6] Rahner is here speaking of the primordial mystery of God which is the heart and unifying centre of all the mysteries of faith – a mystery before which reason must give way and which remains infinite and incomprehensible even for the blessed in heaven.[7] Further elements in Rahner's understanding of mystery will be taken up later in this paper, but from the outset it is important to note the primordial sense in which Rahner is using the term.

2. The Presence of Mystery in the Human Experience of Self-Transcendence

In his most systematic work, *Foundations of Christian Faith*, Rahner's point of departure for his understanding of human existence as grounded in, and oriented to, mystery is an analysis of human knowledge. Highlighting an all too common misunderstanding of the process of knowing, he observes:

> We often imagine the essential nature of knowledge after the model of a tablet on which an object is inscribed, whereby the object comes from outside as it were, and appears on the tablet. We imagine

knowledge after the likeness of a mirror in which some object or other is reflected.[8]

This is the 'image' or 'copy' theory of knowledge taken for granted by what is called 'naïve realism,' the notion that knowledge is simply a matter of looking at what is out there. However knowledge is a much more complex process than this view suggests. When we know something, argues Rahner, we are present both to ourselves and to the data of sense perception. Furthermore this presence to self of the knower is not a static but a dynamic presence, a drive or desire that points out beyond the actual object of knowledge to a larger horizon, indeed an unlimited horizon.[9] This is what Rahner terms the transcendental element in our experience as knowers – 'something which goes on, so to speak, behind the back of the knower, who is looking away from himself and at the object.'[10]

This transcendental element, this implicit orientation to an unlimited horizon, is found in all human activities, in our questioning and questing, our willing and loving. We are restless, dynamic beings, always moving towards a larger horizon, always on the way:

Man can try to evade the mysterious infinity which opens up before him in his questions. Out of fear of the mysterious he can take flight to the familiar and the everyday. But the infinity which he experiences himself exposed to also permeates his everyday activities. Basically he is always still on the way. Every goal that he can point to in knowledge and in action is always relativised, is always a provisional step. Every answer is always just the beginning of a new question. Man experiences himself as infinite possibility because in practice and in theory he necessarily places every sought-after result in question. He always situates it in a broader horizon which looms before him in its vastness.[11]

The restlessness of the human spirit and its constant striving to actualise and realise itself has a social dimension which propels history towards a destination beyond itself:

Man is spirit, achieving consciousness, thinking about himself; and he is history, involved in perpetual change. And because he is both, he can fulfil his nature only by reflecting on the historical situation in which he is placed and which is propelling him forward towards God's eternity, so that in thus reflecting on himself as historically conditioned, he actuates his spiritual being and thus, at the same time, propels his own history towards its destination.[12]

However, while open to a horizon of ever expanding possibilities for self-actualisation in history, the human subject also experiences itself as 'dependent and radically conditioned'.[13] It cannot realise in the world and in history all its possibilities envisaged by its capacity for self-transcendence. Human beings are subjects whose origin and end remain hidden from themselves, and whose ultimate fulfilment has to be received as a gift.[14]

3. The Horizon of Holy Mystery as the Ground and Goal of Human Self-Transcendence

Rahner insists again and again that this infinite horizon which is the term of the human experience of transcendence 'is always present as nameless and indefinable, as something not at our disposal'.[15] It cannot be named because 'this name would situate the term among the realities which are understood within the horizon of this term and this source'.[16] It:

> is indefinable because the horizon itself cannot be present within the horizon, because the term of transcendence cannot itself be brought within the scope of transcendence and thus distinguished from other things. The ultimate measure cannot be measured. The limit by which everything is 'defined' cannot itself be defined by a still more ultimate limit. The infinite expanse which can and does encompass everything cannot itself be encompassed.[17]

Rahner is hesitant to identify the term and source of our transcendence as 'God' and he prefers to speak of it as 'Holy Mystery'.[18] Too often God is thought of as one existent alongside other existents, a member of the larger household of all reality. 'Anyone searching for such a God,' says Rahner, 'is searching for a false God.'[19] The term 'Holy Mystery' better conveys the idea that we are speaking about a reality 'that can never be situated within our system of coordinates, and can never be defined by being distinguished from something else'.[20] The word 'mystery' connotes the idea that the ultimate term of human transcendence cannot be named or defined, and the term 'holy' (although Rahner uses other terms such as 'gracious' and 'absolute' as well) is appropriate since this ultimate term is the condition of the possibility, not only of our knowing, but also of our freedom and love. 'For what else would we call that which is nameless, that at whose disposal we exist and from which we are distanced in our finiteness, but which nevertheless we affirm in our transcendence through freedom and love, what else would we call this if not "holy".'[21]

For Rahner, all human beings, if they are open and attentive, can experience this ultimate horizon of being, this 'Holy Mystery', which we more usually call God:

> Whether he is consciously aware of it or not, whether he is open to this truth or suppresses it, man's whole spiritual and intellectual existence is oriented towards a holy mystery which is the basis of his being. This mystery is the inexplicit and unexpressed horizon which always encircles and upholds the small area of our everyday experience of knowing and acting, our knowledge of reality and our free action. It is our most fundamental, most natural condition, but for that very reason, it is also the most hidden and least regarded reality, speaking to us by its silence, and even whilst appearing to be absent, revealing its presence by making us take cognizance of our own limitations. We call this God.[22]

Rahner goes on to spell out the possibility of a loving graced relationship with this ultimate term of our self-transcendence, experienced as holy and gracious mystery:

> However hard and unsatisfactory it may be to interpret the deepest and most fundamental experience at the very bottom of our being, man does experience in his innermost history that this silent, infinitely distant holy mystery, which continually recalls him to the limits of his finitude and lays bare his guilt, yet bids him approach; the mystery enfolds him in an ultimate and radical love which commends itself to him as his

salvation and as the real meaning of his existence
(provided that he allows its possibilities to be greater
than his own finitude and guilt). This love –
experienced as the ground of being, which is nothing
other than God's absolute self-communication, in
which God gives himself and not only what is finite, in
which he becomes the infinitely wide horizon of our
being – we call divinizing grace.[23]

Here we touch on one of the cardinal principles of
Rahner's theological anthropology, namely, God's primordial
self-communication to humanity constituting a 'supernatural
existential' or graced relationship

offered to everyone as light and as the promise of
eternal life, working freely and graciously in every
person, welling up from the origin of our existence and
– even though not perhaps named as such – appearing
everywhere, where in the history of humankind
courage, love, faithfulness to the light of conscience,
endurance of darkness by faith in the light, or any other
witness to the ground of our being is at work and is
made plain as the holy mystery of the loving nearness
of God.[24]

This means that, for Rahner, our actual human nature, by
virtue of the divine self-communication, transcendentally given
from the very beginning in the ground of human subjectivity,
'is nature in a supernatural order, which human beings (even the
unbeliever and the sinner) can never escape from; nature
superformed by the supernatural saving grace offered to it. And
these "existential facts" of our concrete (historical) nature are
not just accidents of our being beyond consciousness but make

themselves apparent in our experience of ourselves.'[25] Rahner states that this grace is offered to all by virtue of Christ and what he has done for us. Hence, all who respond to this grace are 'anonymous Christians', i.e., without realising it they are embraced by the salvific action of Christ. Our present Pope would seem to be endorsing Rahner's viewpoint when he writes in *Redemptoris Hominis* that 'the human person – every person without exception whatever – has been redeemed by Christ; and Christ is in a way united with each person, without any exception whatever, even if they are not aware of this' (no. 14).

The categorical explicitation and deepening of the mystery of God and his self-communication to us contained in salvation/revelation history is not then 'the unveiling of something previously hidden, which ... leads to an awareness similar to that found in ordinary knowledge of the world. Rather, it means that the *"deus absconditus"* becomes radically present as the abiding mystery.'[26] The history of revelation does not, so to speak, draw back the curtains and remove the mystery. Rather, it heightens and intensifies our involvement with holy and gracious mystery:

> In the history of revelation, the mystery is not removed by a slow process of attrition; rather all the provisional realities are dismantled which can lead to the belief that we can only achieve a relationship to God through what we believe we know about him. But such knowledge only offers figures and images, either good or bad, which represent and shape him to our needs. This process only lasts until we finally let go of everything in the assurance that God, the one who fundamentally cannot be shaped to our needs, becomes through his self-gift the being who alone is fitted to us.[27]

Our final destiny as creatures oriented to, and graced by, holy mystery is to abandon the quest for understanding and yield in love to the unfathomable mystery of God. While Christian revelation may be said to bring out more clearly and to intensify the transcendental experience of God as Holy Mystery, the mystery of God is deepened not dissolved, and we are led ultimately beyond the desire to understand to the contemplation of the incomprehensible silence of God. The following passage from a homily by Rahner on St Thomas Aquinas dramatises the pathway we are all invited to follow:

When we speak of Thomas as a mystic we do not mean that he had frequent ecstasies or visions or that he was a little introverted or overly concerned about his own experiences. There seems to be nothing of this in his writings. Yet Thomas was a mystic. He knew about 'the hidden Godhead', *Adoro te devote, latens deitas* (Devoutly I adore thee, hidden Deity). He knew the hidden God. He spoke of the God who pervades and determines everything in silence. He spoke of a God beyond everything holy theology could say about him. He spoke of the God he loved as inconceivable. And he knew about these things not only from theology but from the experience of his heart. He knew and experienced so much that in the end he substituted silence for theological words. He no longer wrote, and considered all that he had written to be 'straw'. As he lay dying, he spoke a little about the Canticle of Canticles, that great song of love, and then was silent. He became silent because he wanted to let God alone be heard in lieu of those human words he had spoken for us.[28]

4. Implications for the Church's Mission in the World

Rahner's understanding of the human subject as self-transcending, historical freedom, oriented to and embraced by God as ultimate incomprehensible mystery has some important implications for understanding the Church's mission in the world. I wish to highlight its implications in two areas that strike me as especially significant today: the socio-political realm of human self-realisation; and the more personal and interior realm of the relationship between contemplation and mission.

a. The Socio-Political Realm

The Church on earth is called to give historical witness to the radical thrust of human freedom towards the God of our absolute future, beyond any human constructs or systems which might prematurely restrict it. As Rahner puts it: 'Christianity is the proclamation of the absolute hope in the absolute future which is God himself. God himself in his unassailable dominion, a dominion which cannot be established by man, wills to be the infinite future of man, infinitely transcending all man could ever plan or fashion for himself.'[29] This hope in God as our absolute future challenges the Church to adopt a critical stance towards the historically given state of any society.[30] 'Such a critical stance,' says Rahner, 'can be radical, patient and courageous; it implies neither a conservative glorification of the present situation, underpinned by ideology, nor a destructive impatience which seeks violent means to force a new world into existence by sacrificing the men of today.'[31]

The Christian's eschatological vision of human life as oriented to God as its absolute future offers a perspective 'from which to criticise and estimate the relative value of all the individual goals which can be planned and set up on the part of man, and they impart to all these the character of the provisional, that which can be transcended, that which is merely transient and that which can be called in question.'[32] The transient realisations of human beings in history are not rendered insignificant by this perspective. 'On the contrary, it is precisely in virtue of this alone – their orientation to God as absolute future – that they achieve their radical importance and their inexorable seriousness.'[33]

For Rahner, then, the Christian affirmation of God as our absolute future, far from undermining the value of our socio-political commitments within history and our efforts to transform the world, provides a perspective which can guarantee their enduring significance and determine their value. This it does in three ways: first, by offering a framework of meaning profound enough to do justice to the complexity of life and to support human efforts at self-realisation and human transformation; second, by functioning as a critical perspective which de-absolutises all historical conceptions and realisations of human existence; third, by providing a positive incentive to human beings in their efforts to transform human life in history. Since God is our absolute future and the ultimate horizon of human freedom, no socio-political achievement, however great, is unsurpassable or beyond criticism. At the same time, precisely because we have an absolute future in God, all our efforts to transform human life within history have enduring value. In Rahner's words: 'The assent to the absolute future of God, and so the recognition of the relative status of these "this worldly" goals, is achieved in the affirmation of these particular goals within history, and not in a mere attitude of discarding them in a flight from the world. And the recognition of their relative status, so far from diminishing their importance actually increases it.'[34]

Rahner's view of the relationship between the absolute future (God) for which Christians hope and human efforts to transform the world seems to me to find an echo in the following statements from Vatican II's *Pastoral Constitution in the Modern World*:

> Far from diminishing our concern to develop this earth, the expectation of a new earth should spur us on, for it is here that the body of a new human family grows, foreshadowing in some way the age which is to come. That is why, although we must be careful to distinguish earthly progress clearly from the increase of the kingdom of Christ, such progress is of vital concern to the kingdom of God, insofar as it can contribute to the better ordering of human society.
>
> When we have spread on earth the fruits of our nature and our enterprise – human dignity, sisterly and brotherly communion, and freedom – according to the command of the Lord and in his Spirit, we will find them once again, cleansed this time from the stain of sin, illuminated and transfigured, when Christ presents to his Father an eternal and universal kingdom 'of truth and life, a kingdom of holiness and grace, a kingdom of justice, love and peace.' Here on earth the kingdom is mysteriously present; when the Lord comes it will enter its perfection (no. 39).

b. Contemplation and Mission

Rahner's vision of human beings as always and everywhere directed towards and embraced by that ultimate horizon of transcendent mystery we call God implies that the Church's mission is not a matter of taking over from, but rather of participating in God's mission. In the light of Rahner's vision, mission is best seen as an encounter with a mystery: the mystery of a missionary God whose love embraces the world and all its inhabitants; the mystery of the Spirit's power present in unexpected places and unsuspected ways; the mystery of people's participation in the paschal mystery in ways we have neither known or imagined.[35] To encounter this mystery missionaries need to look, to contemplate, to discern, to listen, to learn, to respond, to collaborate.

One of the main challenges facing missionaries is to seek out and discern where and how God's Spirit is present and active among those to whom they are sent, and this is essentially a contemplative exercise. Only a contemplative spirit will enable us not to impose our own agendas on the already existing dialogue between God and people, but rather to enter into this dialogue with the heart and mind of Christ and thus discover God's agenda. Only in prayer can we learn to respect the freedom of God who is present and active among people before our arrival, and to respect the freedom of the people who are responding to God in their own way.

The modern missionary movement was marked by a tragic divorce between contemplation and mission. It has been said, perhaps jokingly, that missionaries asked the contemplatives to do the praying for them while they got on with the task of preaching the Gospel and establishing the Church. But prayer should be seen as an intrinsic, not an extrinsic, dimension of mission. It is only in prayerful contemplation that missionaries are able to attune themselves to God's missionary agenda. Apart from prayer, there is a grave risk that missionaries become propagators of a Gospel that is not of Christ and builders of a Kingdom that has nothing to do with the Reign of God. God's missionary agenda can only be gleaned from a profound listening to the Spirit who has plumbed the depth of God and knows God's ways.

There is an urgent need for missionaries today to retrieve something of that unity of contemplation and apostolic action that marked the monastic missionary movement of the Middle Ages. In the judgement of David Bosch, 'it was because of monasticism that so much authentic Christianity evolved in the course of Europe's dark ages and beyond ... In the midst of a world ruled by the love of self, the monastic communities were a visible sign and preliminary realization of a world ruled by the love of God.'[36] Fortunately, *Redemptoris Missio* has gone some way to correcting the divorce between the missionary and contemplative apostolates by describing the missionary as a 'contemplative in action' (no. 91), thus underlining the intimate relationship between action and contemplation in the life of the missionary. If, according to Rahner, the Christian of the future will either be a mystic or nothing,[37] it is even truer that the missionary of tomorrow will be a mystic or will not exist at all.

Notes

1   Cf. Karen Kilby, *Karl Rahner: Theology and Philosophy*, London: Routledge, 2004.

2   See Endean's review of Kilby's book in *The Tablet*, 23 October, 2004, p. 24.

3   *Ibid.*

4   Karl Rahner, 'The Concept of Mystery in Catholic Theology' in Gerald A. McCool, ed., *A Rahner Reader*, London: Darton, Longman & Todd, 1975, p. 111.

5   'The Concept of Mystery,' pp. 112-114.

6   *Ibid.*, p. 114.

7   Cf. 'The Concept of Mystery in Catholic Theology,' *TI* 4, pp. 50 ff.

8   *FCF*, p. 17.

9   *FCF*, pp. 19-20.

10   *FCF*, p. 18.

11   *FCF*, p. 32.

12   Karl Rahner, *Mission and Grace*, vol. III, London: Sheed & Ward, 1966, p. 24.

13   *FCF*, p. 42.

14   *FCF*, p. 43.

15   *FCF*, p. 61.

16   *Ibid*.

17   *FCF*, p. 63.

18   *Ibid*.

19   *FCF*, p. 63.

20   *FCF*, p. 61.

21   *FCF*, p. 66.

22   'The Need for a Short Formula of Christian Faith,' *TI* 9, p. 122.

23   *Ibid*., pp. 122-123.

24   *Ibid*., p. 123.

25   Karl Rahner, *Nature and Grace*, London: Sheed & Ward, 1963, p. 35.

26   'The Hiddenness of God,' *TI* 16, p. 238.

27   *Ibid*., p. 239.

28   Karl Rahner, 'Thomas Aquinas: Monk, Theologian, and Mystic' in Albert Raffelt and Harvey D. Egan, ed., *The Great Church Year: The Best of Karl Rahner's Homilies, Sermons, and Meditations*, New York: Crossroad, 1993, p. 313.

29   'The Function of the Church as a Critic of Society,' *TI* 12, p. 239.

30   'The Hiddenness of God,' *TI* 16, p. 242.

31   *Ibid*.

32   'The Function of the Church as a Critic of Society,' *TI* 12, p. 239.

33   *Ibid*.

34   *Ibid*., p. 240.

35   Cf. *FCF*, pp. 115-116.

36   David Bosch, *Transforming Mission*, New York: Orbis Books, 1991, p. 230.

37   'Christian Living Formerly and Today,' *TI* 7, pp. 3ff.

II.

Theology in a New Context

The Contributions of Rahner and Lonergan to the Renewal of Theology after Vatican II

CHAPTER THREE

Expanding Lonergan's Legacy: Belief, Discovery and Gender

—— Cynthia Crysdale ——

It is now one hundred years since Bernard Lonergan was born and twenty years since his death. Several generations have now learned 'the basic Lonergan' in the course of their philosophical or theological studies – willingly or unwillingly. If one were to ask any of those students what the core contribution of Lonergan's work has been, you would most likely hear the word 'epistemology' (from the more sophisticated) and something about 'experiencing, understanding, and judging' (from the merely initiated). Generally, Lonergan is remembered for having done work on how we know and, from this, having developed a method in theology.

While Lonergan's work has been met with a mixture of responses, from erudite philosophers who take him to task about linguistic theory to postmodern scholars who would emphasize the situatedness of all knowledge, a review of such critiques is not warranted here. Rather, I wish to highlight Lonergan's legacy by emphasizing an element often neglected by Lonergan's followers: the role of belief and acquired knowledge. This tends to be an underdeveloped aspect of Lonergan's work. I would like to highlight the dialectic between what I call 'heritage' and 'discovery' and then develop it with regard to issues of gender, returning to the very basic Lonergan notion of 'self-appropriation'.[1]

1. Heritage and Discovery

Let me begin with the basic elements of Lonergan's epistemology – the way of discovery. Lonergan's work exhibits the modern turn to the subject in contemporary theology by focusing on theology as an on-going process rather than as a permanent achievement. He shifts the focus in theology from a set of doctrines and principles to a process of questioning and discovery. This process yields cumulative and progressive results and involves a method that, rather than being a set of rules to be followed blindly, is a framework for creativity.[2]

Lonergan claims that human consciousness is divided into distinct types of operations, which occur spontaneously to yield cumulative and progressive results. At a primary level, there is *experience*, which is the mere data of our five senses or that arises from our consciousness itself (memories, images, previous insights, knowledge gained through trusting others). This experience is the matter with which two further types of operations are engaged. First, through questions for *understanding*, an individual comes to discern some intelligible, coherent pattern in the evidence at hand. If, while listening to a lecture, one hears a beeping sound, one spontaneously tries to make sense out of the experience – it could be a cell phone, a pager, a fire alarm, or a garbage truck backing up. All of these lend coherence to what is otherwise a merely coincidental set of sounds.

Still, even a quick read of the options above reveals that not all of these possibilities can be correct. Beyond questions for understanding, there is the innate quest to understand *accurately*. So, in addition to experience and understanding, human persons seek to make *judgments* among the array of possible explanations discovered in the data. Based on the empirical grounds of the experience at hand (or held in memory), we come to the point where some explanations are ruled out of court while others become more and more likely. If enough evidence is available, so that any further questions we have on the matter dry up, we can determine clearly – yes, there is a fire alarm sounding in the building.

Beyond questions of fact, we routinely are involved in another set of questions, having to do with value and *deliberating* on how we should act. Sometimes these questions come first, leading us to seek out the facts. Other times a judgment of fact sets the question for deliberation: having determined that there is, indeed, a fire alarm sounding in the building, I question what action I should take: Jump out the window? Run down the hallway towards the nearest stairwell? Do nothing, assuming that I am safest where I am? Regardless of the concrete situation, the fact remains that, distinct from yet related to determinations of fact, we spontaneously engage in questions of evaluation: What should I do?

While much more could be said to refine and expand on this position on human consciousness, a few salient points can be noted here. First, there is the spontaneity of human consciousness in noticing the world around (and within) us and in seeking to understand it and act upon it. The key word is spontaneity – though older generations may teach us the tools of inquiry and train us in the refinement of our queries, no one needs to tell us to ask questions about, to wonder at, to try to make sense of our worlds. Second, these operations are progressive and cumulative in their effects. The answer to one set of questions leads to a new set of questions. These questions in turn can affect the kinds of evidence we seek or pay attention to. The isolation of a gene related to breast cancer will provide hints as to the proteins that inhibit or promote cancer growth. Understanding how these proteins function in living cells will further narrow the range of possible genes involved in certain cancers. So, the dynamism of human consciousness is energised by a native wonder which, when satisfied, spurs on and contributes to further investigation.[3]

There is an utterly fundamental point here – that the human person is an agent of discovery: she both knows and creates her world. Nevertheless, this dynamism and discovery is only a portion of the story. Lonergan gives an important hint in this regard in several of his later articles. In 'Healing and Creating in History' he refers to two different kinds of development – that 'from below upwards' and that 'from above downwards':

> For human development is of two quite different kinds. There is development from below upwards, from experience to growing understanding, from growing understanding to balanced judgment, from balanced judgment to fruitful courses of action, and from fruitful courses of action to the new situations that call forth further understanding, profounder judgment, richer courses of action. But there is also development from above downwards. There is the transformation of falling in love: the domestic love of the family; the human love of one's tribe, one's city, one's country, mankind; the divine love that orientates man in his cosmos and expresses itself in his worship.[4]

This hint points towards the fact that, in addition to discovery and the innate unfolding of the human capacity to know and create, there is the pre-existing family, tribe, city, state, religion into which every person is born. We are born into a set of cultural meanings that are given to us long before we act upon or create our own meanings. This 'givenness' needs to be taken into any account of human consciousness lest our understanding of moral and cognitive agency be lopsided.

In another article Lonergan speaks of both development and the handing on of development:

> Development may be described, if a spatial metaphor is permitted, as 'from below upwards': it begins from experience, is enriched by full understanding, is accepted by sound judgment, is directed not to satisfaction but to values ... [T]he handing on of development ... works from above downwards: it begins in the affectivity of the infant, the child, the son, the pupil, the follower. On affectivity rests the apprehension of values. On the apprehension of values rests belief. On belief follows the growth in understanding of one who has found a genuine teacher and has been initiated into the study of the masters of the past. Then to confirm one's growth in understanding comes experience made mature and perceptive by one's developed understanding.[5]

This recognition of two aspects of development has its counterpart in the research of the human sciences. The cognitive-structural theories of Piaget, Kohlberg, and others document stages in the way of discovery.[6] On the other hand, psychologists such as Norma Haan and Albert Bandura began in the 1960s to study the role of social interaction in moral formation. Heirs to both behaviourist and Freudian theory, the 'social learning school' created experimental situations in which the role of social interaction in affecting behaviour could be observed. Haan concluded that social dissonance was as formative as cognitive dissonance.[7] Bandura developed the notion of 'modeling' and showed that, even at a preconscious level, we learn moral behaviours through observing and imitating authority figures and/or significant others.[8]

In sociology this work has its counterpart in theories of socialization. Symbolic interactions not only pass on knowledge but create identity as children become social agents in a given context. Perhaps none have captured this important aspect of socialization as well as Berger and Luckmann in their classic work, *The Social Construction of Reality*:

> The primary knowledge about the institutional order is knowledge on the pretheoretical level. It is the sum total of 'what everybody knows' about a social world, an assemblage of maxims, morals, proverbial nuggets of wisdom, values and beliefs, myths, and so forth ...[9] Knowledge, in this sense, is at the heart of the fundamental dialectic of society. It 'programs' the channels in which externalization produces an objective world. It objectifies this world through language and the cognitive apparatus based on language, that is, it orders it into objects to be apprehended as reality ...[10] Again, the same body of knowledge is transmitted to the next generation. It is learned as objective truth in the course of socialization and thus internalized as subjective reality.[11]

Note the parallels here with Lonergan's 'development from above'. In this case development works from the social group to the individual. Rather than beginning with some experience that initiates a set of questions, the person is drawn, through affectivity, to the acceptance of certain values. The infant, the son, the pupil, the follower, is attracted to someone (or group) at the affective and pre-theoretical level. Through this attraction, the person ascribes to his mentor, teacher, parent, friend, or social institution, a great deal of value. On this positive evaluation rests belief. Out of trust the child or pupil accepts as true whatever his parent/mentor or social world tells him. Truths are handed down and accepted out of love, affection, and loyalty. Explanations of truths are equally accepted as given, not because of the logic of the explanation but due to fidelity to the one doing the explaining.

An important point is at stake here. Though much of what we know and value we have discovered for ourselves, Lonergan and others are here pointing out that a good deal, if not most, of what we know and value, we receive from others. In addition to 'immanently generated knowledge' there is the 'knowledge born of belief'.[12] The genesis of this knowledge and these values lies not in the innate questioning of the human person but in the primordial intersubjectivity of persons. We 'fall in love' and thus accept as true and valuable what our loved ones tell us (or model for us).

Thus, in order to adequately understand moral formation or cognitive development, one has to recognize two aspects of the unfolding of human character. On the one hand the upward dynamism of innate curiosity is operative. On the other hand, and at the same time, there are the dynamics of culture as given – the transmission of meaning and value through an equally innate intersubjectivity. These two phenomena operate under the same schema of distinct types of consciousness – Valuing, Judging Truth, Understanding, and Experiencing – only in different 'directions'. One movement is driven by love, loyalty, and commitment while the other finds its impetus in curiosity and the 'pure desire to know'.[13]

What I want to emphasize here is that while Lonergan's legacy may at first blush have to do with his work on the role of insight and judgment in knowing, he makes an equally important, though less developed, contribution to our understanding of what some would call the 'sociology of knowledge'. His position on knowledge as belief and the communal nature of knowledge is most salient in a chapter on the Human Good in *Method in Theology* and two points need to be repeated here.[14] First, belief is not only a factor in moral development, as the social science example above would indicate, but plays an enormous role in the natural sciences. Let me quote Lonergan on the point:

> Science is often contrasted with belief, but the fact of the matter is that belief plays as large a role in sciences in most other areas of human activity. A scientist's original contributions to his subject are not belief but knowledge ... But it would be a mistake to fancy that scientists spend their lives repeating one another's work. They do not suffer from a pointless mania to attain immanently generated knowledge of their fields. On the contrary, the aim of the scientist is the advancement of science, and the attainment of that goal is by a division of labor. New results, if not disputed, tend to be assumed in further work. If the further work prospers, they begin to be regarded with confidence. If the further work runs into difficulties, they will come under suspicion, be submitted to scrutiny, tested at this or that apparently weak point.[15]

This seemingly obvious point has enormous significance in response to common assumptions left from the legacy of the

Enlightenment. Many generations have assumed that science got at the 'facts' while religion dealt with 'belief' – a much less reputable form of knowledge. But in fact, it turns out, even science depends a tremendous amount on what scientists believe and, hence, on the authenticity of the believing subject and the veracity of the authorities he or she believes.

This, then, gets at the second important point with regard to knowledge as belief. The role of belief in knowing reveals that knowledge is a communal endeavour, though indeed dependent on the individual subject. Again, I quote Lonergan:

> Human knowledge, then, is not some individual possession but rather a common fund, from which each may draw by believing, to which each may contribute in the measure that he performs his cognitional operations properly and reports their results accurately. . . No doubt, this public fund may suffer from blindspots, oversights, errors, bias. But it is what we have got, and the remedy for its short-comings is not the rejection of belief and so a return to primitivism, but the critical and selfless stance that, in this as in other matters, promotes progress and offsets decline.[16]

2. Where are the Women?

I have attempted thus far to bring out an aspect of Lonergan's legacy that is often overlooked – the role of belief in knowledge and, thus, the dialectic in human development, as well as in human history, between 'heritage' and 'discovery'. The role of belief leads to the recognition of the communal nature of knowledge, and the social construction of not only what we know but how we know.

The decades that saw the emerging importance of Lonergan's work (*Method in Theology* was published in 1972) were also the early post-Vatican II decades – a period of renewal in the Roman Catholic Church. This same period saw the emergence of women decrying their invisibility in religion. The women's liberation movement of the sixties found its way into the academy and the church in the early seventies. Women's Studies programs proliferated and the critique of patriarchy in religion began in force.[17] Since then feminist perspectives have been brought to bear on almost every aspect of religion, from liturgy and sacraments, to images of God, sexual ethics, Christology, and biblical interpretation. While attention has shifted from critique to retrieval and renewal, one of the areas of concern for feminists has been the social construction of knowledge and the ways in which women have been excluded from public discourse. Common beliefs about who is a knower and who can contribute to the public fund of knowledge have left women on the margins as merely 'receivers' rather than generators of knowledge. In the early 1980's Daniel Maguire claimed that the feminist turn in ethics was primarily about how we know:

> Feminism is concerned with the shift in roles and the question of the rights that have been unjustly denied women. But all of that, however important and even essential, is secondary. The main event is epistemological. Changes in *what* we know are normal; changes in *how* we know are revolutionary. Feminism is a challenge to the way we have gone about *knowing*. The epistemological *terra firma* of the recent past is rocking and as the event develops, it promises to change the face of the earth.[18]

While Lonergan himself never engaged directly with such feminist questions, his extensive work on epistemology might offer something to this revolution. I would like to highlight a few basic points, developing the outline of heritage and discovery as a way of illuminating some feminist grounds for knowing.

First, Lonergan's elucidation of the 'way of discovery' is foundational and, indeed, crucial to the feminist cause. Lonergan is a critical realist, which is to say that he espouses the view that 'reality' can be known and known accurately. The knowing of this reality is a critical endeavour and involves the active operations of the knowing agent. Further, the verification of these operations and their efficacy in knowing depends, not on surveys of every 'Tom, Dick, and Harry,' or 'Sally, Sue, and Sophie' but in self-appropriation, by attending to one's own attending, understanding, judging and deciding.[19] One can generalize this fact to other human subjects by observing their operating and, while one does not have direct access to the structure of others' knowing, one has to acknowledge and account for the communication and collaboration that revolves around attention to experience and the quest for intelligibility, truth, and value. Finally, this concretely universal and unrevisable fact can provide a rock upon which any inquiry, and any articulation of the method for that inquiry, including feminist method, can be built.

This 'self-affirmation of the knower',[20] while some feminists may find it solipsistic, is crucial to the feminist cause because it empirically grounds the structure of human consciousness and its ability to know reality. This common ground is what makes conversation, communication, debate possible. It is the basis on which women can legitimately make the claim that they too, in spite of centuries of cultural messages to the contrary, are capable of knowing. An affirmation of this critical realism is the basis for insisting that women's voices should be heard. Women, just as well as men, the poor as well as the rich, the educated as well as the disenfranchised, all spontaneously ask questions and seek to understand their worlds. The 'pure desire to know' is not a privilege of the elite, nor is it a commodity, over which affluent white men have a monopoly. Lonergan's critical realism, as affirmed in the self-appropriation of the subject herself, provides a foundation for establishing basic human rights – the dignity of being heard, the right to learn, to question, to speak, to be taken seriously. Without such an affirmation of this universal structure to human consciousness, the claims of women and other minorities can be dismissed as irrational, a-rational, intuitive, emotive, or otherwise not worthy of attention.[21]

Thus Lonergan's epistemology can ground the commonality of human knowing across gender, race, and class. What about the differences? Most feminists have been loath to affirm a common way of knowing since this so often in the past has meant a hegemony of the élite: those with power determine what knowing and knowledge is, and any alternative voices are marginalised as deviant. Feminists have tended to emphasize *women's* ways of knowing, as a 'different voice' that has been silenced and now needs exposure.[22] I believe that this is where Lonergan's discussion of belief becomes so important. The crucial point is this: one set of beliefs into which all persons are socialized is a set of beliefs about knowing itself. The work of feminists has pointed out that the Western European cultural tradition has handed on a legacy in which women are considered non-knowers. At best women have been considered 'receivers' but not 'generators' of knowledge. In a sense, then, men have been seen as the 'discoverers' of knowledge, while women have been relegated to the 'heritage' side of the equation.

Let me invoke Lonergan directly, as he speaks about belief and how one deals with erroneous belief systems:

> (W)hen one makes a discovery, when one comes to know what one did not know before, often enough one is advancing not merely from ignorance to truth but from error to truth. To follow up on such discovery is to scrutinize the error, to uncover other connected views that in one way or another supported or confirmed it. These associates of the error may themselves be errors. They will bear examination. In the measure they come under suspicion and prove to be erroneous, one can move on to their associates and so make the discovery of one error the occasion of purging many. It is not enough, however, simply to reject errors. Besides the false beliefs there is the false believer. One has to look into the manner in which one happened to have accepted erroneous beliefs and one has to try to discover and correct the carelessness, the credulity, the bias that led one to mistake the false for the true. Finally, it is not enough to remove mistaken beliefs and to reform the mistaken believer. One has to replace as well as remove, to build up as well as tear down. Mere hunting for errors can leave one a personal and cultural wreck without convictions or commitments. By far the healthier procedure is primarily positive and constructive, so that what is true more and more fills out one's mind and what is false falls away without leaving a gap or scar.[23]

It is precisely this process in which the women's movement has been engaged over the last several decades. Women have begun to question certain truths implicit in the traditions they received, for example, that anatomy is destiny or that children will be psychologically damaged if their mothers work outside the home. Among others, economic structures, theological doctrines and medical practices have been examined to unveil inequities and distortions. Furthermore, the process of raising consciousness regarding patriarchy has involved not only pointing out single errors but also naming the bias, uncovering the blindspots that have led to these errors. Finally, the reconstruction of new sets of meanings that are free of patriarchal bias has taken place in reference to many facets of personal and communal life.

It is here that I would place the role of women's studies and the scholarship of gender. The task of uncovering false beliefs, discerning false believing and reconstructing new and more accurately defined facts and values involves shifting from the way of belief and heritage to the way of discovery, of beginning to judge and decide for oneself which beliefs are valid and which are distorted. What is new, then, in the women's movement and in feminist scholarship is not a gender specific process of knowing but the unveiling of patriarchal bias in the facts and values that both women and men have received in the way of heritage. Most important, among the distortions that have been handed on through a patriarchally biased tradition are distortions about the process of knowing itself. In particular, the educational system, the economic system, and family patterns of communication have impressed upon women a role of passivity in regard to knowing. Women have traditionally been receivers of knowledge. They have rarely been in positions economically, socially, or culturally to generate their own knowledge.

It is not surprising, then, that women have become experts in the knowledge born of belief. They are very familiar with the relational connections, the affectivity that generates trust, the love and trust that leads to accepting the values of the beloved, to endorsing the judgments of another, to adopting the explanations given and to moulding experience according to these accepted beliefs. They have also become experts at passing on knowledge through generating love and trust in others and by appealing to this relational base as a legitimate source of knowledge.

Now, as I have been at pains to point out, the idea that knowledge involves belief and that believing can be a valid way of gaining knowledge, is essentially sound. But the idea that believing is the only access that women have to knowledge is a distortion born of prejudice. The notion that women cannot participate in the way of discovery, that they are unable to have insights, to make verifiable judgments, or to discern and create value comes from bias rather than sound judgment. In fact, the eros of discovery is just as operative in women as it is in men. It is only distorted and biased tradition that has overlooked or hidden this fact.

3. Self-Appropriation and Social Location

In the last several decades, several social scientists have documented the developmental patterns evident in certain groups of American women. Carol Gilligan's *In a Different Voice* became an instant success when published in 1982. Later in that same decade Belenky, Clinchy, Goldberger and Tarule set out to gather evidence about how women from a variety of social locations understood their own understanding.[24] The study by Belenky et al. reveals a pattern in which women move from silence to the discovery that they can learn through others ('received knowledge') to the discovery that their own inner voice can contribute to the knowing process ('subjective knowledge'). Some women moved past this stage to realize that their inner voice can at times be wrong and to learn the role that objective reason plays in knowing ('procedural knowledge'). The final stage that these researchers outline involves the integration and interplay between the criteria of the inner voice and the need to attend to outer reality ('constructed knowledge').

These studies illustrate and confirm several of the points I have been making here. They illustrate the important role of belief, of received knowledge in which one accepts truths and values determined by others. One of the most striking points revealed here is the relationship between self-concept and theories of knowing. Women who had very little power in the world not only had low estimates of themselves but also described the knowing process as very passive, as something to which they contributed very little.[25] As women had opportunities to learn and as they actually engaged in the way of discovery, they began to challenge their dis-empowered roles. Conversely, the more women became empowered in their social situations the more they were able to articulate the process of discovery in which they engaged. Thus the stories of these women are stories of self-appropriation, of the growing ability of these women to understand their social circumstances, to critique both the content and process by which they had come to accept distorted truths and to objectify the process of discovery itself.

What becomes particularly evident in examining the trends in 'women's ways of knowing' is that the distorted beliefs that have and still do oppress women are precisely beliefs about believing and discovery themselves. Historically, to the degree that women were considered cognitive agents at all, they were relegated to believing what others told them.[26] Many contemporary women, if they are not totally 'silent,' can only conceive of themselves as receivers of knowledge. Even those who move beyond this to some confidence in their own 'inner voice' find assertion of their role as 'discoverers' of knowledge to be radical and revolutionary, requiring courageous changes in their communities of meaning. Thus, self-appropriation for women, even in its descriptive, un-technical form, seems to engage them in powerful existential struggles, not only with regard to the operations they use in knowing, but with their roles as agents of their own discoveries rather than as mere receivers of others' knowledge.[27]

The implications of this discovery of agency are manifold. With regard to Lonergan's foundational position regarding self-appropriation, it means that what is implicit in Lonergan's thought needs to be made explicit. And it is precisely this: that self-appropriation involves not only verifying a particular set of operations as basic to what is involved in immanently generated knowledge. Self-appropriation also involves distinguishing clearly between the knowledge of discovery and the knowledge born of belief and, regarding the latter, heightening one's awareness of assumptions about knowing itself. This is not to deny but to enhance the power of Lonergan's critical realism. Surely to attend to and affirm the fact that one knows not by 'looking' or by imagining but by experiencing, understanding, and judging is most basic. But just as basic is the affirmation that, in addition to the myth that 'knowing is like looking' there is the myth that 'knowing is merely hearing', that is, that merely believing others is the only route open to knowledge.

With regard to women's lives it becomes apparent that 'self-appropriation' can be a powerful tool for liberation. At the same time this analysis reveals clearly the 'conditions of possibility' for such a self-appropriation to take place. Basic material resources and structural opportunities are necessary before women can even begin to conceive of themselves as cognitive agents.[28] A community of dialogue in which language is seen as a tool for communication seems fundamental. Related to this is the absence of violence and/or the threat of violence.[29] It seems clear that the experience of benign authorities is necessary before any appropriation of reasoned discovery can take place. Most obviously, the full flowering of 'reason' (over against subjectivism) seems only to occur when opportunities of higher education are available: the inequality of 'life chances' promoted by classism and racism cannot be overlooked. Yet even the experience of the 'benign' authorities of higher education seems to be tainted with either the reality or fear of sexual harassment. The overwhelming presence of sexual abuse or harassment among women of all epistemological perspectives is surely a central factor. To the degree that self-appropriation of oneself as a knower is dialectically related to appropriation of oneself as a believer, and to the degree that authentic believing rests on trustworthy authorities, the absence of 'safe' environments for women is a key obstacle to their self-appropriation. The presence of trustworthy female mentors, in a variety of contexts, seems directly tied to women's discovery of discovery.

4. Conclusion

There is no doubt that Lonergan's legacy lies in what he himself would call Foundational Theology. His epistemology, that is, his critical realism grounded in the self-affirmation of the knower, has provided a rock upon which he and now others have built an explicit theological method. The implications of both this epistemology and this method have still to be mined to their depths. My task here has been to bring out an often overlooked aspect of Lonergan's work in an attempt, first, to fill out the contribution Lonergan has made to our understanding of knowing and, second, to develop this fuller model in terms of women's ways of knowing and the feminist questions raised in the last four decades.

Experiencing, understanding, judging, and deciding as the four levels of operations basic to human consciousness: this is the 'basic Lonergan' and many have been challenged (and should still be challenged) to identify these operations in themselves and verify the recurrent pattern that leads to knowledge of the world around and within us. But much of what we 'know' comes not from these operations but from our trust in others' previously generated knowledge. In addition to the 'way of discovery' there is the 'knowledge born of belief' or 'the way of heritage'. Such inherited knowledge has its flaws, blindspots, and prejudices, just as immanently generated knowledge can be infiltrated with mistakes that need to be corrected. Nevertheless, the dialectic between heritage and discovery is ever with us – eliminating bias is a matter of critical engagement in our discovering and our believing.

With regard to women's ways of knowing there is a complex answer to the question, 'Do women have a distinctive way of knowing?' On the one hand, the self-appropriation of the knower leads to the important point that everyone is capable of discovery – and Lonergan's critical realism is a strong ally in defence of women's claim to cognitive parity. At the same time, a critical reading of Western cultural history reveals that for centuries women have been regarded as receivers rather than generators of knowledge. The positive aspect of this is what one might call the 'ethics of care' – women have and can contribute to society through distinctive patterns of loyalty, affectivity, trust, and belief – fostering the community of knowledge. The negative side of this is that such 'received knowledge' has often been denigrated and that women have been restricted to being told by others what is true, good, or beautiful. The various feminist movements of the last two hundred years could be described as 'the discovery of discovery' by women in an Enlightenment world. Once women began to realise that they could discover things for themselves, the right to contribute to, rather than merely pass on, the public fund of knowledge became the battle to be waged – in the polling booths, in the family, in the workplace, and in religious spheres.

Such 'discovery of discovery' continues today. My final point in this paper is that the implications of such self-appropriation cannot be left to philosophers and theologians in ivory towers. For many, many people, the discovery of cognitive agency goes hand in hand with a radical and even dangerous existential claim to autonomy. It is tied in to political, economic, psychological, and religious structures that are oppressive; claiming personal agency as a discoverer necessarily puts some in the position of challenging centuries-old prejudices and injustices. The intellectual conversion discussed by Lonergan is not only a matter of overcoming the myth that knowing is like looking. It also involves contradicting the myth that knowing is only a matter of hearing. And while many see Lonergan's legacy as erudite but obscure, realising these implications of his work makes self-appropriation anything but a merely academic exercise. For some, if not for all, true cognitive self-appropriation is an act of courage, faith, and sacrifice.

Notes

1   This essay integrates ideas expressed in a number of articles already published by the author. See Cynthia S. W. Crysdale, 'Gilligan's Epistemological Challenge: Implications for Method in Ethics,' *The Irish Theological Quarterly*, 56 (1990), pp. 31-48; 'Women and the Social Construction of Self-Appropriation,' in Cynthia S.W. Crysdale, ed., *Lonergan and Feminism*, Toronto: University of Toronto Press, 1994, pp. 88-113; and 'Heritage and Discovery: A Framework for Moral Theology,' *Theological Studies* 63 (2002), pp. 559-78.

2   See Lonergan, *Method*, 'Introduction.' What counts here is not just what Lonergan says about theology and theologians, but that his work on theological method presents a basic anthropology of human discovery. He does not rely on observation and experiment in the way of the social sciences, but uses a generalized empirical method to show that human persons are dynamically oriented towards interacting with, understanding, and changing their worlds. All persons, he claims, use the same pattern of recurrent and related operations to interact with their worlds. This pattern can be verified, not by observing 'every Tom, Dick, and Harry,' but through each person being attentive to what they are doing while they are doing it – what Lonergan calls 'self-appropriation'. For the reference to 'Tom, Dick, and Harry,' see Bernard Lonergan, *Insight: A Study of Human Understanding*, New York: Harper and Row, 1957, p. xviii. On 'self-appropriation', see Lonergan, *Method*, pp. 6-7, 13-16, 83-85.

3   Note that Lonergan's 'levels' of operations, here described, are not the same as 'stages' in a theory of human development. The operations that Lonergan outlines function myriad times in a single day, are cumulative, progressive, and repetitive. 'Stages' as outlined by developmental theory serve as benchmarks over a much longer time span. A person moves through the stages only once, and cannot go back and repeat stages of thought, whereas the operations Lonergan elucidates are necessarily repetitive – the operations occur over and over again, while the content (what one is asking about or seeking to understand) changes depending on the situation.

4   Lonergan, 'Healing and Creating in History,' 3C, p. 106.

5   Lonergan, 'Natural Right and Historical Mindedness,' 3C, pp. 180-181.

6   See Jean Piaget, *The Moral Judgement of the Child*, New York: Penguin Books, [1932] 1977; Lawrence Kohlberg, *The Philosophy of Moral Development*, San Francisco: Harper and Row, 1981; and James Fowler, *Stages of Faith*, San Francisco: Harper and Row, 1981. For a recent discussion of these theories in relation to moral theology, see William C. Spohn, 'Conscience and Moral Development,' *Theological Studies* 61 (2000), pp. 122-38.

7   See Norma Haan, Elaine Aerts, Bruce A. B. Cooper, *On Moral Grounds: The Search for Practical Morality*, New York: New York University Press, 1985.

8   See Albert Bandura, *Social Foundations of Thought and Action: A Social Cognitive Theory*, Englewood Cliffs, NJ: Prentice Hall, 1986. See also Joan E. Grusec, 'Social Learning Theory and Developmental Psychology: The Legacies of Robert Sears and Albert Bandura,' *Developmental Psychology* 28 (1992), pp. 776-89. Both Haan and Bandura are discussed in Timothy E. O'Connell, *Making Disciples: A Handbook of Christian Moral Formation*, New York: Crossroad, 1998, pp. 79-82, 91-94.

9   Peter L. Berger and Thomas Luckmann, *The Social Construction of Reality: A Treatise on the Sociology of Knowledge*, New York: Doubleday, 1966, p. 65.

10   *Ibid.*, p. 66.

11   *Ibid.*, p. 67.

12   See Lonergan, *Method*, pp. 41-47. This section, entitled 'Beliefs' begins with the following sentence: 'To appropriate one's social, cultural, religious heritage is largely a matter of belief'. Many scholarly fans of Lonergan's work have been so taken with his epistemology (of 'discovery') that this aspect of Lonergan's thought has been often overlooked. One exception would be Frederick E. Crowe, *Old Things and New: A Strategy for Education*, Atlanta: Scholars Press, 1985. It is Crowe from whom I have borrowed the term 'heritage' to designate one aspect of development and to whom I am indebted for inspiring many of the salient ideas here.

13   Note that, in either direction, the whole thing is driven by affectivity. While Lonergan's work has often been portrayed as overly cognitive, to the neglect of the affective dimensions of

consciousness, the entire process of discovery and learning is grounded in the pure *desire* to know.

Note further, there is a certain chronology here. The way of heritage is our socialization into culture and is most operative in infancy and childhood. An infant, while curious, even prior to language development, is most dependent on the world around her to provide not only sustenance but also affection. This affection becomes the ground of trust from which the child, through symbols, fantasy, play, and questioning, learns to exercise her tools of discovery. But while these tools of discovery are emerging the child depends on the knowledge gained by being told. Developmental theory bears this out – for the young child truth and goodness lie in authorities external to themselves. Until the child reaches the 'age of reason' and learns to think for himself, meaning and value, reality and morality, are defined by the powers that be in his world.

As childhood progresses, all other things being equal, the child learns the tools of discovery and learns how to use them to discover truth and value for herself. So the primary focus of development moves gradually from the way of heritage to the way of discovery. Still, the 'age of reason' is elusive and a strict chronology does not adequately define the relationship involved. While at young ages heritage and socialization are more operative, and while the pendulum gradually swings towards the greater autonomy of discovery and achievement, the two processes are never separate, nor does one replace the other. Rather, the two movements fall into a dialectical relationship, which Lonergan describes as involving 'linked but opposed principles of change'. See Lonergan, *Insight*, pp. 217ff.

14   Lonergan, *Method*, pp. 41-47.

15   *Ibid.*, p. 43.

16   *Ibid.*, pp. 43-44.

17   For a review of gender studies and their emergence in university curricula, see Anne Carr, *Transforming Grace: Christian Tradition and Women's Experience*, San Francisco: Harper and Row, 1988, pp. 63-94. See also Anne E. Patrick, 'Women and Religion: A Survey of Significant Literature, 1964-1974,' *Theological Studies* 36 (1975), pp. 737-65. Some basic early critiques include: Rosemary Ruether, *Religion and Sexism: Images of Women in the Jewish and Christian*

Tradition, New York: Simon and Schuster, 1974; Letty Russell, *Human Liberation in a Feminist Perspective*, Philadelphia: Westminster Press, 1974; and C. Christ and J. Plaskow, eds., *Womanspirit Rising*, San Francisco: Harper and Row, 1979.

18   Daniel C. Maguire, 'The Feminist Turn in Ethics,' *Horizons* 10 (1983), p. 341.

19   See Lonergan, *Insight*, p. xviii; *Method*, pp. 6-7; 13-16; 83-85.

20   See Lonergan, *Insight*, chap. 11.

21   See Cynthia S. W. Crysdale, 'Horizons that Differ: Women and Men and the Flight From Understanding,' *Cross Currents* 44 (1994), pp. 345-361.

22   See Carol Gilligan, *In a Different Voice: Psychological Theory and Women's Development*, Cambridge, MA: Harvard University Press, 1982.

23   Lonergan, *Method*, p. 44.

24   Mary Belenky, Blythe Clinchy, Nancy Goldberger, and Jill Tarule, *Women's Ways of Knowing: The Development of Self, Voice, and Mind*, New York: Basic Books, 1986.

25   One relation that stands out clearly here is that between violence in the family and a sense of passivity or helplessness in learning. The majority of women who were silent or at the stage of 'received' or 'subjective' knowledge had some experience of familial violence in their past. Violence did not seem to be as common in the experience of women at the higher stages of 'procedural' or 'constructed' knowledge. See Belenky et.al., *Women's Ways*, pp. 32, 56-7, 158-60, 180.

26   Loraine Code, in a review of the history of women's roles in public knowledge, says the following: 'Excluded from public intellectual debate, woman is more restricted than 'real' members of the epistemic community to reliance upon testimony *chosen for her*: to the tutelage of her patrons, friends, and lovers. Her possibilities for circumspection are fewer than those available to men. Hence the distance she can acquire from her own cognitive endeavours to cast a critical eye upon them… and the scope of her possible epistemic responsibility is, accordingly, narrowed. She is *more than* naturally reliant upon acquiring knowledge from others, … more at the mercy of those she is *permitted* to trust, than is man, who at least is *in a position* to choose more widely, however well or badly he may do this.' From 'Responsibility and the

Epistemic Community: Woman's Place,' *Social Research* 50 (1983), p. 547.

27 Note that though my emphasis here is on the move beyond received knowing, Belenky et.al. indicate that there is a sort of 'self-appropriation,' which is very liberating, when women move from silence to the rudimentary discovery that they can *receive* knowledge. An example is the story of Ann, whose experience of childbirth catapulted her into a need to learn. Her introduction to the workers at the social agency who seemed to know everything she needed to know regarding babies was a very profound experience. Note that their provision of knowledge was combined with a confidence in Ann's own intellectual abilities, a combination that served to change Ann's life. See Belenky et.al., *Women's Ways*, pp. 35-36.

28 See Alison Moore's study of the relation between basic social and material resources and women's conception of themselves as moral agents: 'Moral Agency of Women in a Battered Women's Shelter,' *Annual of the Society of Christian Ethics*, (1990), pp. 131-47. See also Belenky and her colleagues' discussion of Liz and Mimi, and how their opportunities to move beyond 'silence' were entirely different owing to their differing socio-economic class. Though both suffered from the sexual abuse of a tyrannical father, Liz managed to transcend her circumstances thanks to financial resources that gave her opportunities to find other sources of strength and growth. Mimi, lacking such resources, reacted by running away from home, an action that ultimately landed her in a detention centre. See Belenky et.al., *Women's Ways*, pp. 160-2.

29 The presence of domestic violence within the lives of the 'silent' women, and even amongst the 'received knowers' is overwhelming. Comparing Moore's study of battered women and their sense of agency with Belenky et. al. (cf. pp. 27-28, 32) makes it clear that there is a profound connection between the socialization of women as *receivers* of knowledge and the social acceptance of violence against women. While teaching women to be receivers of knowledge has value in itself, restricting them to this role, while appearing benign, may in fact have tragic social implications. The flip side of this connection is that asserting one's ability to discover one's own truth presents a

direct challenge to the (sometimes violent) power that men wield in women's lives. Thus, Lorraine Code's allusion to the courage required for a woman to assert herself as a knower is no mere conjecture but has its concrete reality: the existential commitment of self-appropriation, alluded to by Lonergan, can put some women at the risk of losing their lives.

CHAPTER FOUR

Karl Rahner's Contribution to Interreligious Dialogue

—— Dermot A. Lane ——

'If we can see further today, it is because we stand on the shoulders of giants.'

Questions about interreligious dialogue, the possibility of a Christian theology of religions, and the reality of religious pluralism are to the fore in theology today – so much so that it can be said that a new way of doing Christian theology has emerged in the last twenty years, and that this was made possible by the previous twenty years during which Karl Rahner was active advancing the agenda of the Second Vatican Council.

The purpose of this paper is to examine Karl Rahner's contribution to interreligious dialogue in the post Vatican II period. To discern this it is necessary to do two things. First of all one must re-read Rahner's theology with an eye on what he had to say indirectly or in passing about other religions, knowing, of course, that there is no such thing as a passing reference in Rahner! Only then in the light of this re-reading is it possible to come to grips with the few articles he wrote dealing directly with interreligious dialogue.

There are four parts to this paper. We will review what Rahner had to say about interreligious dialogue indirectly through the development of basic themes. Secondly, we will examine some of his writings on the relationship between Christianity and other religions. Thirdly, we will engage in a critical evaluation of Rahner's contribution to this theme. Finally, we will outline what a Christian theology of interreligious dialogue might look like going forward in the company of Karl Rahner.

1. Themes in Rahner's Theology Shaping His Understanding of Interreligious Dialogue

Clearly there are many themes in Rahner's theology that have shaped his understanding of other religions and all that can be done here is to select some, but not all, of these basic themes. The themes chosen include the experience of God, grace, revelation, the person of Christ, and anonymous Christianity – all of which have a direct bearing on Rahner's contribution to interreligious dialogue.

a) The Experience of God

The theme of the experience of God is at the centre of Rahner's entire work. What is distinctive about Rahner's theology of experience is his claim that everybody experiences God, even though they may deny this, or may not be consciously aware of it, or may choose to interpret it non-theologically.[1] Rahner rescues the experience of God from being something peculiar to saints, the preserve of mystics, or the privilege of the few. When it comes to describing the experience of God he consistently uses terms like 'ineffable,' 'inexhaustible,' and 'incomprehensible'.

Concerning the mystical experience of God Rahner seems to go beyond his own principles. In a few exceptional cases he talks about the immediate experience of God and describes this as imageless,[2] occurring without concepts, and going beyond words in a way that entails encounter with God's own self.[3] In struggling to account for this kind of experience Rahner refers to the 'phenomena of a non-Christian spirituality and mysticism and also many descriptions of Christian mystical experiences'[4] as a warning against dismissing the possibility of the immediate experience of God.

Grace

The next theme is grace – the key that unlocks the richness of Karl Rahner's thought. He introduces his theology of grace by giving priority to what he calls 'uncreated grace' in contrast to the scholastic emphasis on created grace.[5] Uncreated grace is about God's self-communication to the human being. Every human being is marked by a divine gracious imprint. This supernatural hallmark is the result of the enduring gift of God's self to every human person. We come into the world 'inwardly determined'[6] as it were by the gracious love of God and this gives everyone a particular disposition, orientation and dynamism turned towards God. The effect of this upon the person is what Rahner calls 'the supernatural existential'.

Other features of grace are that it is mediated though the great diversity of human experience and is ultimately Christological, given in virtue of Christ who is the fullness of God's self-communication to humanity and the perfect expression of humanity's response to this divine gift. This doctrine of grace has a profound influence on the way Rahner approaches other religious traditions.

Revelation

The third theme of revelation flows out of Rahner's theology of grace. The story of the unfolding of the grace of God in the world is the history of revelation.[7]

Rahner develops, on the one hand, what he calls the universal, transcendental aspect of revelation and, on the other hand, the categorical, historical aspects of revelation. The transcendental aspect of revelation is the result of Rahner's theology of grace and as such only makes sense within that specific context. Transcendental revelation is available not as an object but as a graced horizon, not as a statement but as a presence, not as a series of propositions but only as a supernatural offer of God's self to all human beings, not as something out there but as a non-objective awareness of God.

On the other hand, there is the categorical, historical aspect of revelation which is about the mediation, objectification, and thematisation of transcendental revelation. This process of expressing transcendental revelation has been going on in history since the dawn of human freedom and can be found in varying degrees in the history of art, culture, science and religion.

d) The Person of Christ
The person of Christ is a major theme in *Foundations* and the *Investigations*. Within his theology of interreligious dialogue, the Christ-event appears as an unsurpassable, unrepeatable, and irrevocable moment within the history of transcendental and categorical revelation. The person of Christ is the absolute breakthrough of God's gracious self-communication to humanity and humanity's free response to God's invitation. For Rahner grace and revelation reach finality in Jesus, the crucified and risen one. The Incarnation stands out as the radiating centre of the whole of Rahner's theology.

One of the many significant moves in Rahner's Christology, consistent with his theology of grace, is the relocation of the Christ-event within the larger history of humanity and other religions. Instead of seeing the Christ-event as an external intervention in history, Rahner insists on presenting the person of Christ as the decisive moment internal to the unfolding of God's universal saving will within the history of the world.

e) Anonymous Christians

Our fifth and final basic theme is anonymous Christians, or anonymous Christianity, a term that caused controversy for Rahner throughout his life.[8] The primary reason why Rahner constructed the idea of an anonymous Christianity was pastoral. How do you account for the very large numbers of people, past and present, who have never heard the good news of Jesus Christ? How are we to make sense of the existence of so much unbelief and what Rahner called 'inculpable atheism' in the world? How do you situate Christianity within the larger context of a world in which two-thirds are non-Christian? To answer these complex questions Rahner comes up with the idea of the anonymous Christian.

2. Explicit Treatment of Interreligious Dialogue

Relative to the four thousand books, articles and reviews that Rahner wrote during his life there are only a few articles dealing directly with interreligious dialogue and even fewer dealing with other religions as such. Indeed it would be wrong to give the impression that interreligious dialogue was at the centre of Rahner's theological enterprise. Instead, it would be more accurate to say that Rahner was passionate about dialogue, dialogue between Christianity and the world, dialogue with atheism, Marxism, unbelievers, scientists, and this is the context in which dialogue with non-Christian religions should be located. Our concern here is with interreligious dialogue and not his treatment of other religions.[9]

His articles on dialogue with the non-Christian religions are few but are no less important in their significance. What is striking about these few articles is that they entail the application of the basic themes we have been enunciating to the particular question of the relationship that exists between Christianity and other religions. I will deal here with some of these articles in the order of their appearance. The articles chosen are selective and do not pretend in any way to be a comprehensive account of everything that Rahner had to say about the relationship between Christianity and the other religions.

The 1961 Lecture

The first and by far the most important and original article on other religions was a lecture given in 1961. In this lecture, unchanged in its published version in 1962, entitled 'Christianity and the Non-Christian Religions',[10] he puts forward four theses with an introduction and a conclusion. He introduces the lecture with comments on an 'open Catholicism' which he says requires the Church to understand what is outside itself. He notes the existence of religious pluralism and sees it as both a threat and a challenge for the Church.

In Thesis (1) he says that Christianity understands itself as an absolute religion which is true and lawful, intended for all, and, therefore, cannot recognise any other religion as of equal right.

In the first half of Thesis (2) he affirms that non-Christian religions 'have supernatural elements arising out of the grace which is ... given as a gift on account of Christ'.[11] As Christians we believe that the universal saving will of God is directed towards all human beings. In the light of God's universal saving will and the Christ-event we must recognise that grace is at work everywhere in the personal lives of people 'no matter how primitive, unenlightened, apathetic and earthbound such a life may appear to be'.[12]

In the second half of Thesis (2) he points out that the pre-Christian religions have 'a positive significance' in history and therefore they must be regarded as 'lawful'[13] provided they have some form of public and institutional existence. A lawful religion is one that can be regarded as 'a positive means of gaining ... the right relationship to God and thus for the attaining of salvation'. Such lawful religions may also be regarded as 'positively included in God's plan of salvation'.[14] While Rahner makes the case for lawful religions principally by reference to the Old Testament it is clear that he also has the other religions in mind.

In Thesis (3) Rahner points out that Christians should not regard members of other religions as non-Christian but rather as anonymous Christians. It would be wrong to regard the pagan as someone who has not been touched by God's grace and truth.

In Thesis (4) Rahner says that religious pluralism is not going to disappear in the foreseeable future. Consequently, it is permissible for the Christian to interpret this non-Christianity as Christianity of an anonymous kind. The role of the missionary is to bring 'to consciousness ... what has already been accepted unreflectively and implicitly'.[15] If we can look at non-Christians in these terms, that is as people already touched by grace, 'then the Church will not regard itself as the exclusive community of those who have a claim on salvation, but rather as the historically tangible vanguard ... and socially constituted expression of what is present as a hidden reality outside the visible Church'.[16]

b) Christ in Non-Christian Religions

In 1974 Rahner published a paper on 'Jesus Christ in Non-Christian Religions' in the *Investigations* which was subsequently incorporated without much change into the *Foundations*. The purpose of this article was to explain how and in what sense it is possible to speak of Christ as present and active in other religions, especially in view of the particularity of the Christ-event. To this question, Rahner responds that Christ is present through the Spirit and that this Spirit is the Spirit of Christ.

A second way in which we can talk about Christ being present in other religions is in and through what Rahner calls 'the searching memory of all faith'.[17] By this he means that within faith there is a searching dynamic looking for the existence of an absolute saviour figure. There is 'a prior principle of expectation, of searching, of hoping'[18] within memory.

c) The Importance of other Religions for Salvation

A third article entitled 'The Importance of Non-Christian Religions for Salvation' was given as a lecture in 1975 to an international congress of missiology in Rome. Are other religions just constructs created by human beings, or can they act as sources of salvation for people? In raising these questions Rahner notes the shift that has taken place from over a millennium of Augustinian pessimism to the new optimism at Vatican II which teaches that salvation is available to all those who do not freely reject it.[19] For Rahner 'non Christian religions, even though incomplete, rudimentary, partially debased, can be realities with a positive history of salvation and revelation.'[20] Such religions can, therefore, have a positive salvific function and become 'ways of salvation' through which people approach God.[21]

One further point in this 1975 lecture worth mentioning is what Rahner says about mysticism: 'it is not a priori forbidden to discover genuine supernatural mysticism in the mysticism of religions of higher cultures, even when this extra Christian mysticism is not ... by any means thematised in an explicit religious form.'[22]

3. Critical Evaluation of Rahner
It is now time to review Rahner's contribution to a theology of interreligious dialogue. It would hardly be true to the spirit of Rahner simply to parrot off what he had to say without some critical engagement.

a) A Pioneer of Dialogue and Inclusivism
In general one can only admire the openness of Rahner's theology to dialogue with other religions and, how, historically speaking, he anticipated in many respects developments that were to take place in the late 1980's and throughout 1990's and into the third millennium. Rahner's theological approach to other religions enabled Catholic theology to effect a number of significant shifts which we now take for granted. These include the shift from an exclusivist theology to an inclusivist Catholic theology, the move from Augustinian pessimism about salvation to the optimism of Vatican II about the salvation of all, and the adoption of a positive approach to other religions in contrast to the largely hostile approach prior to Vatican II.

b) Examination of the Basic Themes
(i) Rahner's theology of the experience of God is extremely rich and his ability to connect the most ordinary experiences of life with the omnipresence of the Holy Mystery is surely striking as a point of departure for

dialogue with other religions. His insistence that the experience of God is an experience of that which is ineffable, inexhaustible, and incomprehensible is also an attractive point of entry into dialogue with other religions.

(ii) Next comes his theology of grace and the supernatural existential which is described by David Coffey as of immense 'importance for reflection on the relationship of Christianity to world religions.'[23] Likewise, Philip Endean observes that Rahner's theology of grace has 'momentous consequences ... for the relationship between Catholic Christianity and the world at large'.[24] It is above all else Rahner's theology of grace that enables him to see other religions as divinely willed by God and therefore a legitimate part of salvation history and a means of mediating a saving relationship with God.

(iii) Concerning Rahner's theology of revelation, it must be acknowledged that his distinction and emphasis on transcendental and categorical aspects of revelation widens the context in which dialogue with other religions can take place. It pushes back the boundaries of revelation beyond the Judaeo-Christian dispensation to the long history of revelation that preceded what is sometimes called the special revelation of the Bible. Rahner's theology of revelation, as one author puts it, 'undermines the Christian imperialism that declares God's revelation to have begun only with Judaism and to have been made perfect only with the Christian Church'.[25]

(iv) Our fourth basic theme concerns Rahner's Christology and its relationship to other religions. His presentation of the Incarnation as the ontological point of contact between God and humanity captures in a very credible manner an important part of what is distinctive about Christianity. This view of the Incarnation, however, needs to be filled out in terms of the historical drama that actually took place within the unfolding of the Incarnation. Even though Rahner, especially the later Rahner, emphasises the importance of history he fails to give much specific material content of history. This neglect by Rahner stands out all the more today because of the prominence given in Christology to the ongoing quest for the historical Jesus. Rahner's transcendental Christology clearly needs to be grounded in a more particularised, historical narrative about Jesus of Nazareth.[26]

(v) The last basic theme in Rahner's theology is that of anonymous Christians. For some this concept appeared to play down the need for explicit faith for salvation, for others it undermined the missionary trust of the Church, and for still others it seemed to water down the uniqueness of the Christian message. These reactions, many of them answered by the later Rahner, fail, it seems to me, to take sufficient account of how his theology of anonymous Christianity is supported by the interlocking basic themes outlined above. To eliminate anonymous Christianity from Rahner's theology one would need to deconstruct the basic themes enunciated in the first part of this paper.[27]

c) His Treatment of Interreligious Dialogue

We now come to an evaluation of Rahner's explicit treatment of the relationship between Christianity and other religions. His 1961 paper was by any standards a most original, creative and influential contribution. The vision of this article has been described as a 'giant leap forward'[28] within Catholic theology at that time. Further, this 1961 article along with the basic themes enunciated enabled Catholic theologians to adopt a positive and inclusive view of other religions which we now take for granted.

Gavin D'Costa has described Rahner as 'probably the most influential inclusivist theologian of the twentieth century'.[29] The inclusivism in question, however, has come in for criticism in recent times. It is pointed out that such inclusivism does not foster learning *about* or *from* other religions because Christians already know in advance what there is to learn about or from other religions. In brief, this inclusivism does not seem to foster real dialogue among the religions.[30]

In response to this criticism it should be noted that Rahner in the sixties was trying to open a closed door through his theology of inclusivism. Further, Rahner's theology of dialogue, used to good effect with atheists and Marxists, does not preclude learning about and from atheists and Marxists, and therefore, it would not be true to Rahner's intention to pre-empt genuine learning about and from other religions.

In addition, this 1961 article paved the way for what is now known as 'inclusive pluralism' within the current state of inter-religious dialogue, a position we will return to in the fourth part of this paper.

The second article dealing with other religions entitled 'Jesus Christ in the Non-Christian Religions' was written in 1974. The issue at stake in this article as we have seen is: how can Christ be present in other religions? Rahner suggests that Christ is present through what he calls the searching memory of faith, a concept which has a curious resonance with some postmodern deconstructionists such as Jacques Derrida which we will also look at in the next part.

In the third article 'On the Importance of Non Christian Religions for Salvation' written in 1975, there is some repetition of themes, more confidence and less qualifications! A striking feature of this article is the seemingly passing reference to the supernatural mysticism of the religions of higher culture, even though this mysticism is non-thematic and without form. This question of mysticism we will take up again in part four.

d) The Transcendental Method

To conclude this critical evaluation of Rahner something needs to be said about his transcendental method. Rahner used the transcendental method creatively throughout his life. Whether the transcendental method is sufficient for a theology of religions operating in a post-Enlightenment, disenchanted world is a major question. I believe that Rahner's transcendental theology is in need of some reform and revision.

It must be acknowledged that in spite of Rahner's best efforts his transcendental theology appears to be caught in some of the ambiguities of modernity, being far more dependent on particular historical and linguistic systems than he acknowledges. Further, what David Tracy says in general about transcendental theology is applicable to Rahner, namely that it 'is too deeply related to the embattled and self-deluding self of modernity'.[31] The self of transcendental theology needs to be far more conscious of itself as a historical subject with a living memory, a subject that is ultimately accessible only in narrative form, and even then every expression in narrative form is incomplete.

A second point about Rahner's transcendental theology is that if the turn to historical consciousness is to succeed, then Rahner's transcendental theology will need a new imagination. This new imagination will have to be more rooted in memory, especially the historical memory of God's healing and empowering action not only in Judaism and Christianity but also within particular moments of the history of the major world religions. When this happens then transcendental theology will be in a position to imagine, or better to re-imagine, how the action of God continues to address humanity and the religions of the world to day. The shape of this re-imagining of God's action will only become apparent in the light of interreligious exchanges.

4. Going Forward in the Company of Rahner in the Context of Interreligious Dialogue

In the fourth and final section I want to outline, briefly, how it is possible to go forward and to see further standing on the shoulders of Rahner in the context of interreligious dialogue. My suggestions at best can only be schematic.

a) Rahner's Theology of Mysticism

The first area I want to highlight is Rahner's complex theology of the experience of God and mysticism. As seen he does refer to non-Christian mysticism and spirituality and to the mysticism of the religions of the higher cultures, leaving open a space, an odd and undefined space, for further dialogue with other religions. While these references to non-Christian mysticism may appear as extravagant rhetoric when read in the context of his fundamental theology, they take on new life when read in the context of interreligious dialogue. It is as if there were three streams of mysticism, three ways of talking about mysticism, in Rahner's theology: one for mainstream Christian theology, one in relation to Ignatius' immediate experience of God, and one which he calls non-Christian mysticism.

In contrast to most commentators, I do not want to iron out these 'odd' references to mysticism in order to integrate them into the mainstream of Rahner's theology. Why? First of all because these references, especially to the possibility of an imageless and formless experience of God, may well resonate with some religions of the East, especially Hinduism and Buddhism. Further, I do not want to play down these references because there is a mystical tradition within Christianity, quite familiar to Rahner, that does talk in these extravagant tones about a direct experience of God and union with God. This odd focus in Rahner on non-Christian mysticism may well act as a bridge for Christians in dialogue with other religions.

b) Rahner and Postmodernism

The next area going forward in the company of Rahner concerns the context within which interfaith dialogue takes place. For those who live in the so-called developed world, that context is inescapably pluralist and postmodern. Rahner recognised the reality of pluralism years ahead of most Catholic theologians. Less obvious is Rahner's relationship with postmodern culture. And yet Declan Marmion rightly suggests Rahner 'anticipated some of the characteristics' of postmodernity.[32] Allowing for the enormous ambiguity and fluidity attaching to the term 'postmodern', one of the agreed features of postmodern culture is its programme of deconstruction, especially in the work of Jacques Derrida.

In a fascinating and unexpected way one finds some echoes of Derridian deconstruction in the work of Rahner.[33] Both engage in a programme of deconstruction without however wanting to eliminate religion; both emphasise the searching and messianic character of experience; both reach out beyond all human, historical and cultural mediations of religion: Rahner by talking about the possibility of an imageless experience of God and Derrida by talking about 'religion without religion'.[34]

A further point of contact between Rahner and Derrida can be found in Rahner's appreciation of apophatic theology and Derrida's radical programme of deconstruction which included what might be called a passing flirtation with negative theology. While Derrida did discern a certain 'family resemblance'[35] between the negations of apophatic theology and deconstruction, he ended up confessing 'I would hesitate to inscribe what I put forward under the familiar heading of negative theology'.[36] In brief, Derrida gave up on the possibility and viability of a negative theology largely because of his suspicion of a latent 'hyperessentialism'. In contrast Rahner's early studies of Gregory of Nyssa and Evagrius as well as his familiarity with Pseudo Dionysius and Meister Eckhart enabled him to affirm and negate the incomprehensibility of God in such a way that he could talk about 'knowing through unknowing'.[37]

The question that must be put to Derrida is: how is it possible to talk about the messianic character of experience without giving it any content and to affirm 'religion without religion'? In the end, Derrida admits, 'nothing remains'.[38] The trouble with this, however, is that you cannot embrace negations, or as Denys Turner puts it, paraphrasing Scotus within a postmodern context, you cannot love a mere postponement.[39]

In spite of these faint echoes, which I believe are significant for interreligious dialogue, it must be pointed out that there is a very substantial difference between Rahner and Derrida. This fundamental difference comes down to Rahner's clear and unambiguous recognition of Jesus of Nazareth as the Messiah and absolute Saviour of the world, a recognition that Derrida refuses of all religions. The other major difference is that Rahner's deconstruction is in the service of reconstruction whereas Derrida brings us to the brink of the abyss and leaves us waiting!

c) Inclusive Pluralism

A third area in which we can go forward in the company of Rahner is in the ownership and development of what has now become known as 'Inclusive Pluralism'[40] – a term used by Jacques Dupuis and Claude Geffré. Rahner's theology of inclusivism paved the way for the development of 'inclusive pluralism' which offers a new perspective on a Christian theology of religions.

For Dupuis inclusive pluralism brings together inclusivism and pluralism in a way that avoids the relativism of radical pluralism and the absolutism of exclusivism. In addition, inclusive pluralism safeguards the uniqueness of the Christ-event for the salvation of the world while recognising the possibility of salvation in other religions through what is called a process of 'participated mediation.'

d) Christianity – An Open and Unfinished Narrative

Our fourth and final area in which we can go forward in the company of Rahner concerns the unfinished and incomplete character of Christian revelation. As we have seen in his discussion about the relationship between the transcendental and categorical aspects of revelation, Rahner points out as a matter of principle that the objectification of revelation 'is only partially successful' and 'always exists within a still unfinished history'.[41] This general principle applies to all forms of categorical revelation, including the objectification of the Christ-event.

One of the most striking features of the self-understanding of the first Christian community of Jews was the acute awareness that there was something still outstanding in their experience of the life, death and Resurrection of Jesus. The unfinished work and incomplete character of the Christ-event is a feature found in the earliest Christologies of the New Testament. One of the clearest expressions of this incompleteness of the Christ-event is given in the early prayer *Maranatha, Come, Lord Jesus* (1 Cor. 16:22). The early church expected the imminent return of Christ to complete what Jesus Christ inaugurated.

Another expression of the unfinished nature of the Christ event is found in some of the Pauline Christologies. There is an underlying tension in Paul's theology between the 'already' and the 'not yet' of the Christ-event, between being 'in Christ' and 'becoming in Christ', between the present and the future. The sense that there is something still outstanding about the Christ-event is also captured by Paul in the language which describes Christ as 'the first fruits' (1 Cor.15:20), 'the beginning of the end' and 'the first born among many' (Rom. 8:29; Col. 1:18).

A further expression of the unfinished character of the Christ event can be found in the doctrine of the second coming of Christ/*Parousia* which not only pervades the New Testament but also the early creeds and liturgical celebrations. David Tracy, for instance, points out that when 'the second coming of Christ...becomes a symbol as important as the symbols of the incarnation, cross and resurrection' then 'the work of Christology will open into a...theological interpretation of Christianity in relationship to other religions'.[42]

In a similar vein Claude Geffré notes it is only a Christianity aware of its own lack that will be able to encounter fruitfully other religions; it is absence and not presence that makes things happen; actions occur more often than not because of what is lacking.[43]

To sum up then, a unique part of Rahner's legacy to theology has been his distinctive contribution to interreligious dialogue. In this he was able, along with others, to stimulate the Second Vatican Council to adopt a positive attitude towards other religions, and, in the post-Vatican II period, he provided dialogical perspectives for development of an inclusive theology of non-Christian religions, which today, in the light of the basic themes outlined at the beginning of this chapter, is able to service the emerging theology of 'inclusive pluralism'.[44]

Notes

1   'The Experience of God Today,' *TI* 11, pp. 149-65 at p. 150.

2   Karl Rahner, 'Mystik-Weg des Glaubens zu Gott,' *Horizonte der Religiosität*, 1978, p.19. I am indebted to Philip Endean's instructive and insightful analysis of this issue in *Karl Rahner and Ignatian Spirituality*, Oxford: Oxford University Press, 2001, Ch. 2.

3   Karl Rahner, *The Dynamic Element in the Church*, London: Burns and Oates, 1964, p. 148.

4   Rahner, *The Dynamic Element*, p. 145, n.34.

5   'Some Implications of the scholastic concept of Uncreated Grace,' *TI* 1, pp. 319-46.

6   'Questions of Controversial Theology,' *TI* 6, pp. 189-218, at p. 200.

7   'History of the World and Salvation History,' *TI* 5, pp. 97-114; See also 'History of Salvation and Revelation,' *FCF,* pp. 138-175.

8   See *TI,* vols. 6, 9, 12, 14.

9   Rahner's best known dialogue with Judaism is contained in *Encountering Jesus-Encountering Judaism: A Dialogue*, New York: Crossroad, 1987 and with Islam in 'Oneness and Threefoldness of God in Discussion with Islam', *TI* 18, pp. 105-121. For a helpful evaluation of Rahner's views on Judaism and Islam see Peter Phan,

'Karl Rahner in Dialogue with Judaism and Islam: An Assessment', in *Religions of the Book*, ed., Gerard Sloyan, The 1992 Annual Publication of the College Theology Society, vol. 38, Washington, D.C.: The University of America Press, 1996, pp. 129-50.

10   'Christianity and the Non-Christian Religions,' *TI* 5, pp. 115-34.

11   *Ibid.*, p. 121.

12   *Ibid.*, p. 125.

13   *Ibid.*, p. 125.

14   *Ibid.*, p. 125.

15   *Ibid.*, p. 133.

16   *Ibid.*, p. 133.

17   *FCF*, p. 319.

18   *Ibid.*

19   'On the Importance of the Non-Christian Religions for Salvation,' *TI* 18, pp. 290-91.

20   *Ibid.*, p. 294.

21   *Ibid.*, p. 295.

22   *Ibid.*, p. 295.

23   David Coffey, 'The Whole Rahner on the Supernatural Existential,' *Theological Studies*, 65 (2004), pp. 95-118 at p. 117.

24   Philip Endean, *Karl Rahner and Ignatian Spirituality*, Oxford: Oxford University Press, 2001, p. 39.

25   *Karl Rahner: Theologian of the Great Search for Meaning*, ed., Geoffrey B. Kelly, Edinburgh: T & T Clark, 1992, p. 128.

26   This neglect of historical detail is noted by Johann Baptist Metz, *Faith in History and Society: Towards a Practical Fundamental Theology*, London: Burns and Oates, 1980, pp. 159-162, and Stephen J. Duffy, *The Dynamics of Grace: Perspectives in Theological Anthropology*, Minnesota: Michael Glazier/Liturgical Press, 1993, p. 311.

27   An up-to-date review and assessment of Rahner's theology of anonymous Christianity is provided by Eamonn Conway in 'So as not to Despise God's Grace: Re-assessing Rahner's Idea of the 'Anonymous Christian', *Louvain Studies*, Spring-Summer 2004 (Essays Marking the Centenary of Karl Rahner's Birth), pp. 107-30.

28   Paul Knitter, *Introducing Theologies of Religions*, New York: Orbis, 2002, p. 68.

29   Gavin D'Costa, 'Theology of Religions,' *Modern Theologians*, ed., David Ford, second edition, Oxford: Blackwell, 1997, pp. 626-44 at p. 631.

30 See James L. Fredericks, *Faith Meets Faith: A Christian Theology of Non-Christian Religion*, New York: Paulist Press, 1999, pp. 32-33.

31 David Tracy, 'Literary Theory and the Return of the Forms for Naming and Thinking God in Theology,' *The Journal of Religion* 74 (1994), pp. 302-319 at p. 305.

32 Declan Marmion, 'Theology, Spirituality, and the Role of Experience in Karl Rahner,' *Louvain Studies*, Spring and Summer (2004), pp. 49-76 at p. 76.

33 One of the first to note this curious echo between Rahner and Derrida was Michael J. Scanlon in 'A Deconstruction of Religion: On Derrida and Rahner,' *God, the Gift and Postmodernism*, eds., John D. Caputo and Michael J. Scanlon, Indiana: Indiana University Press, 1999, pp. 223-28.

34 Jacques Derrida, 'Faith and Knowledge: The Two Sources of "Religion" at the Limits of Reason Alone,' *Acts of Religion*, edited with an introduction by Gil Anidgar, London: Routledge, 2002, pp. 40-101.

35 Jacques Derrida, 'How to Avoid Speaking: Denials,' in Harold Coward and Toby Foshay, eds., *Derrida and Negative Theology*, New York: State University of New York Press, 1992, p. 74.

36 *Art.cit.*, p. 78.

37 Endean, *Karl Rahner and Ignatian Spirituality*, pp. 22-23, who is quoting from Rahner's *Aszese und Mystik in der Väterzeit*, Freiburg: Herder, 1938.

38 Jacques Derrida, *On the Name*, California: Stanford University Press, 1995, p. 51.

39 Denys Turner, 'Apophaticism, Idolatry and the Claims of Reason,' *Silence and the Word: Negative Theology and the Incarnation*, eds., Oliver Davies and Denys Turner, Cambridge: Cambridge University Press, 2002, p. 34.

40 This particular concept of inclusive pluralism has been put forward by Jacques Dupuis in *Christianity and the Religions: From Confrontation to Dialogue*, New York: Orbis Books, 2002, pp. 87-95 and has been defended by Dupuis in "Christianity and the Religions' Revisited,' *Louvain Studies* 28 (2003), pp. 363-83. This concept is also found in the writings of Claude Geffré. See, for example, Claude Geffré, 'The Christological Paradox as a Hermeneutic Key,' *Who Do You Say I Am: Confessing the Mystery of*

Christ, eds., John Cavadini and Laura Holt, Indiana: University of Notre Dame Press, 2004, pp. 155-72.

41   *FCF*, p. 173.

42   Scott Holland, 'This Side of God: A Conversation with David Tracy,' *Cross Currents*, 52 (2002), pp. 58-59.

43   Claude Geffré, 'Christological Paradox as a Hermeneutical Key to Inter-Religious Dialogue,' *Who Do You Say I Am: Confessing the Mystery of Christ*, eds., John Cavadini and Laura Holt, Indiana: Notre Dame University Press, 2004, pp. 167-68. Geffré is drawing here on the work of Michel de Certeau.

44   I am grateful to Professor Terrence Tilley of the University of Dayton who read an earlier version of this paper and made helpful suggestions for its improvement.

III.

The Situation of Theology in Contemporary Ireland

CHAPTER FIVE

Theology in Ireland: Changing Contours and Contexts

—— Eamonn Conway ——

Introduction

It struck many people as strange that a topic such as this, a particularly broad and general one, would be chosen as the keynote address at a major symposium to honour the lives and work of Bernard Lonergan and Karl Rahner. Yet, as we have seen from the papers specifically exploring aspects of the work of these theological giants, life and work do not separate easily, and theological reflection always takes place in a context. So do conferences. This is a time of profound change for theology in Ireland, change that is driven by a number of factors, some of which we will consider here. It is important for us to step back from the particularity of our theological engagement, look at the shifting landscape, and identify a set of markers by which we can plot the most appropriate course for theological engagement into the future.

I have chosen to explore this topic under the following headings. Following these introductory comments I will consider pragmatism as characteristic of the Irish way of doing theology, and the merits and demerits of this. I will then argue for theology as essentially an *ecclesial* activity and as an *essential* ecclesial activity. I will then attempt to explore the particular challenges facing theology as third-level education in Ireland undergoes profound change, before concluding with some observations regarding opportunities as well as dangers that we face in the near future.

When I returned from studying theology in Germany in the early 1990s, I remember being struck by the extraordinary richness and variety of the Irish theological landscape. In Germany, even though I lived and worked in a parish while studying, I experienced a certain chasm between the pastoral and the academic, and a carefully ordered hierarchy by which engagement in theology was valued, with the parish community assistant at the lower end of the hierarchy and the university professor at the higher.

We regret the fact that theology in Ireland has not found until recently, with very few exceptions, much hospitality in third-level institutions. However, I believe that this institutional homelessness has contributed to theology here being more open, creative and inclusive. This is something to be cherished. Later in this paper I will be focusing on the issue of theology and the university (meant in the broadest sense of third-level). However, I will not mean or wish to play down the significance of the 'loving reflection on the wisdom carried to us in the community' (James Mackey's definition of theology), which takes place actually *in* believing communities, by believers engaged in the front-line renewal of the Christian community.

1. Reflection v Transformation, and the Issue of Pragmatism

In the early nineties, the Irish Theological Association sponsored some reflection on Irish theology. At that time, John O'Donohue wrote that 'the only carriers of theology in Ireland have been and still are the clerics', who fed people what they got themselves (Sebastian Moore would add, 'in concentrate'!): 'a theological algebra… ingested from theological tracts at the seminary.'[1] When O'Donohue was writing we still had seminaries in the plural in Ireland, though they had already begun to languish. Now, significantly, even the Dutch Church has more seminarians than Ireland, and all but one of our seminaries have either adapted or died. More if still not many lay people are formally employed in teaching theology here today, and new centres have emerged, such as the Western Theological Institute in Galway, and the Newman Institute in Ballina. And theology, or at least its accreditation, has made significant in-roads into third-level institutions, ironically in the younger universities (Dublin City University, University of Limerick) and the Institutes of Technology, especially in Galway and Waterford.

In the early nineties, theologians in Ireland were concerned with a different set of social problems. Emigration was still running quite high; we could not have even considered that immigration and multi-culturalism would become challenges and opportunities for us. There was concern about the North of Ireland. Poverty and social exclusion were also major issues of concern. Although perhaps they should, these questions do not tend to dominate our discussions today.

One particularly interesting question was raised at that time, one arguably that is still with us, though I think the contours have changed. The question related to what I might call the 'pragmatic' nature of Irish theology: the issue of whether or not theologians viewed their role primarily as a matter of reflection, or as one of transformation. The question was posed as to whether theology 'commits (theologians) to work for a just, participative, sustainable society, or is their task merely to reflect on and analyse society from a Christian standpoint?'[2] The question was loaded: it expressed an annoyance among some ITA members at the absence of theology from Irish public life and its apparent distance from pressing social concerns. At the same time, in his contribution, Werner Jeanrond expressed the view that Irish theologians suffered from 'a mélange of middle-class guilt' and 'salvific illusion' which affected their ability to engage in 'ethical and self-critical theological thinking'.[3] Along similar lines, O'Donohue was suspicious (rightly) that 'relevance questions' often mask prior questions about identity.

There is always tension between patient, critical, scholarly theological reflection, and concrete public engagement with both social and ecclesial realities. And despite our tendency towards pragmatism, which some would see as a national characteristic, reflected socio-economically in our greater proximity to Boston than to Berlin, it is significant and regrettable, that we never really developed an indigenous Irish theology of liberation.

Those who are primarily engaged in one or other form of transformative ministry probably still sense the frustration expressed in the nineties about theology failing to take seriously its situatedness. They would probably remind us that 'the family, the parish, the community or the school is what it is all about. If you do not speak out of and into these contexts you are only speaking to yourselves'. In order to survive, but also in order to serve, many former seminaries have developed attractive interdisciplinary programmes that provide people in ministry with the skills to engage with, and be influential in, the new Ireland. Later I argue that the insight, creativity and sheer ingenuity shown by former seminaries give them a critical decisive edge in a new educational context.

However, others here would tend to agree with Jeanrond, and perhaps be even more concerned now than he was a decade ago. This would be because of the increasing reality that theological teaching and research is almost entirely determined by what has to be done in order to attract students so that institutions can survive. And most Irish theologians have to teach in areas outside their interest/specialism in order to have any employment at all.

'Pure' theology, whatever that is, does not sell all that well in Ireland. Pragmatism determines that we offer courses with at least one or preferably all of the terms 'spirituality,' 'pastoral' and 'ministry' in order to attract students. Whereas I suspect the dominant fear in the early nineties was that theology was not sufficiently cognisant of its social responsibilities and sufficiently committed to social transformation, today I suspect a fear many of us share is that, well-grounded, historically conscious, scholarly reflection is under threat. Instead of 'publish or perish' it is a case of 'produce student numbers or perish'.

I have a two-fold concern regarding the nature of this newer kind of 'pragmatism'. Instead of having the merit of the earlier kind which at least was overtly committed to social transformation, this newer kind can be more self-centred, and this in two ways. It can be focused on the self of the institution in order to guarantee its survival, or it can be focused upon the self of the individual, in order to lead to personal fulfilment. In both cases the focus of transformation runs the risk of being self-centred and self-serving. Of course it doesn't have to be, and there are plenty of examples of ways that it is not. In the business world nowadays one speaks of 'win-win' situations, where both society as a whole and companies 'profit' from certain business strategies. Perhaps what is needed here is careful reflection on the part of all the 'stakeholders' on what can be 'win-win' situations for institutions, individual scholars and students, the Church, society and the discipline of theology as a whole. I believe we face a real dilemma here, one which I experience in my own current context which is a state-funded university-college: principles are acceptable insofar as we can afford them.

The dilemma is compounded further by the fact that we are marked, as Timothy Radcliffe has put it, 'by a culture which has lost confidence that study is a worthwhile activity and which doubts that debate can bring us to the truth for which we long'. It would be wrong for us simply to capitulate to this culture. At the same time, our scholarliness should not and need not be at the expense of service. Our Church and our culture need, which is not to say that they necessarily want, theology. They need to hear and see and experience theology in a whole variety of contexts. So, to summarise: one issue for theology in contemporary Ireland is how to negotiate between survival, service and scholarship, engaging with yet challenging the exigencies of contemporary culture.

2. Theology as Essentially an Ecclesial Activity

It is accurate to say that until recently most formal theological instruction took place in seminaries. And some of the criticisms of this kind of theology have to be taken on the chin. Its urgency to instruct rather than explore, its failure to honour and engage the uniqueness of the Irish imagination, its absence from public discourse, support O'Donohue's assertion that Irish theology 'was trapped somewhere in the tottering presbytery of Irish clericalism' for quite some time. Significantly, however, and ironically, those most articulate in unveiling the inadequacies of this kind of theological formation are themselves products of it. Somehow, despite the shallowness of the soil and at times poor tilling, or maybe too much, seeds were sown and propagated in those seminary seedbeds, seeds that have since yielded significant harvests. Some very gifted people on the staff in these seminaries paid a price for this, often living and working in an oppressive and at times cruel and personally diminishing institutional environment, and they held onto and even communicated an understanding of redeemed humanity despite the odds. Indebtedness to these people should not be forgotten as we hasten on to graze in new and perhaps more exciting and personally fulfilling theological pastures.

The fact that theology in Ireland in the past was undertaken mainly by priests and in seminary contexts does not mean that it was necessarily undertaken as an ecclesial activity or that it served the *ecclesia* well. It certainly was possible to undertake theology in the seminary and be engaged in scholarly reflection that was so removed from the life of the Church that, while it was not *sentire contra ecclesiam*, (a thinking/feeling *against* the Church), it was hard to justify it as a genuine and valuable *sentire cum ecclesia* (a thinking/feeling *with* the Church).

Nonetheless, the migration of theology from church-controlled seminary contexts to institutions with merely formal ecclesiastical control such as university integrated denominational Colleges of Education and the Liberal Arts where I work, or to Institutes of Technology, where no formal control is possible except the control one can exercise over individual lecturers, raises questions about whether we understand or wish to understand theology as essentially an ecclesial activity. This is an important question, and one that is particularly difficult to address because it relates to questions of authority, power, control, trust, freedom, and even employment and livelihood.

We will return to the issue of the universities. First, I want to explore further the question of theology as an ecclesial activity. I believe that theology is essentially and inherently an ecclesial activity. While theology is responsible to and must correlate with the three publics of which David Tracy spoke, the Church, the academy and society, it does so as a particular representation of and manifestation of a wisdom which is embodied in and resides in a believing community. Anything else is really a form of philosophical or sociological study, valuable and interesting in itself, but distinct. I want to quote Mackey's definition of theology, to which I referred earlier, in full:

> a loving reflection on the wisdom carried to him/her in the community, in its life and literature, its liturgy, its developing structures and its mission; using in this task the God-given gifts of the imagination and intelligence: the critical power of being able to distinguish the better embodiments of wisdom and the worse; the visionary power to envisage, however dimly, what would be better still; and such clarity and cogency of expression as would make this life-work a true core-summation of the religious tradition for a particular time and place.

There are understandable reasons as to why some theologians would find this understanding of theology a challenge they would prefer to pass on. Occasionally, critical powers to discern and point out the better embodiments of wisdom and the worse have been greeted with suspicion and even hostility, and some theologians are simply 'tired' of been merely 'consulted' if not entirely ignored when it comes to urgently needed reforms regarding liturgy and the structures and mission of the Church. It is particularly annoying when reforms are governed by pragmatic considerations alone, and experts in all sorts of other areas are consulted (at great expense), while a theological opinion is not sought after. It is a sad reality that nowadays one finds that the academy and society in Ireland take theologians more seriously than Church authorities.[4]

There are other reasons as to why theologians might wish to shed the ecclesial mantle. For example:

- they do not wish 'to sink with the institutional ship';
- they may believe a distancing from the magisterium to be necessary if theology is to find acceptance within the university;
- they may find certain doctrinal positions relating to 'hot potatoes' such as mandatory celibacy, ordination of women, homosexuality etc., untenable, and do not want to be a part of defending them or even exploring them;
- they still fear the control that the magisterium might be able to or attempt to exercise;
- they may be actually convinced of the validity of a Religious Studies methodology along the lines developed by Ninian Smart, and of its appropriateness in the contemporary Irish cultural context.

Nevertheless, I would argue that:

- Theology is essentially an ecclesial activity. It is, as Mackey says, 'a loving reflection' on the wisdom that resides in a believing community. People in love see things differently. I know it is said that 'love is blind.' At the same time, love opens up horizons and possibilities to which the dispassionate and disengaged are oblivious. I think we can only do theology if we are in love with the tradition, faithful to it, and in some sense humbly subject to it. This may mean at times being critical of certain positions, but always in a spirit of humility and of service. If we are genuinely in love with the tradition, we can say, with St John of the Cross, 'where you do not find love, put in love, and you will draw love out'.

- If we do not consider theology as an ecclesial activity, it is hard to see how we can hold in creative and critical tension the dual responsibility of theology to be both reflective and transformative. There is great emphasis today on knowledge. We speak of the knowledge economy, and we aspire to being a knowledge society. However, knowledge of itself is not transformative. Only faith, hope and love transform. Religious Studies may increase our knowledge, but only theology, I would argue, increases our faith, hope and love. An increase in faith, hope and love are needed by all three of theology's constituencies: the Church, the academy and society. Information is not enough, what is needed is transformation.

There are more pragmatic reasons as to why we should continue to view theology as an ecclesial activity:
- The reality is that many of the institutions that offer theology programmes and employment opportunities are Church sponsored. It is simply appropriate that theology is undertaken as an ecclesial activity in these contexts.
- Most of those who wish to study theology in Ireland may have deep faith questions as well as troubled and troubling experiences of Church. But, for the most part, they wish to engage in theology as an ecclesial activity.
- Most of our graduates, if they find employment, will find employment in Church-related institutions and be

expected to undertake theological reflection as an ecclesial activity.

Of course, we run the risk of narrowness and inwardness if we do not also speak of theology as essentially ecumenical at the same time as speaking of it as essentially ecclesial. I cannot develop this here, but I think it is important that we explore the new ecumenical and inter-faith challenges and responsibilities in multicultural Ireland. If we do not, we will not be serving our students well.

Finally, as we honour Rahner and Lonergan, it is appropriate to remind ourselves that neither of them could have conceived of theology as anything other than ecclesial. Both of their lives are testimony to a certain kind of theological being-in-love. In *Insight*, Lonergan urged us to 'convert' from self-satisfaction to value as the criterion of our decision-making and action. This could be said to apply in particular to our decision as to whether or not we wish to view theology as an ecclesial activity.

When considering the future of theology, Rahner acknowledged that it would have to be far more pluralist, but he also urged that 'it would discover in a fresh and more living way that ecclesiological element which is proper to it and which belongs permanently to its nature'.[5] He argued that as theology rightly takes seriously the individual's own faith and sense of truth, it is all the more important that this individual sense of faith and truth is related to community, society and Church as socially constituted. Otherwise, 'it will never achieve its due fullness ... allowed to wander alone in the isolated sphere of private opinion.'

3. Theology as an Essential Ecclesial Activity

Theologians need no convincing that theology is an *essential* ecclesial activity. However, at least some Church authorities might need theology more than they appear to want it. We have seen many failed pastoral initiatives in Ireland, and in my view this is because of insufficient theological reflection. These initiatives have shown signs of being born of a 'pastoral panic', and have often taken the form of programmes imported from other cultural contexts without sufficient reflection upon or recognition of the uniqueness of our own socio-cultural and ecclesial context.

A satisfactory spirit of collaboration between bishops and theologians does not yet exist in Ireland. Yet I know that quietly, many bishops and religious superiors fund lay students to pursue theological studies, and have been doing so for years. It would be good to see more being done to create jobs in theology for these people once they graduate. It would also be good to see bishops encouraging and facilitating their personnel in engaging in continuing theological renewal; indeed it would be great to see bishops engaging in it themselves. It would also be a step forward if there was more consultation and discussion between bishops and theologians, especially before pastoral letters are issued or pastoral policies put in place.

Finally, I think that quiet, patient 'backroom' scholarly theological reflection needs to be be supported more, and this in very practical ways, in terms of resources, sabbaticals etc. Vincent Twomey, in his recent book, *The End of Irish Catholicism?*, laments the fact that scholarly research and publication tends to take second place to teaching and administration.[6] The fact is there is no ideal context for doing theology, and wherever we find ourselves, we will be struggling to make time and give value to research and reflection. Some of us by personality will be more disposed to it than others, but we will all find it easier to engage in lonely and solitary scholarship if it is supported by and valued by the *ecclesia*.

Symbolic rewards have a place for theologians. It is easy to censure a theologian who is perceived to have erred. It would also be nice to honour and encourage those who are viewed to have made a significant contribution to theological scholarship.

4. Theology and the University

a) Working without state funding

One of the key issues facing many of the places where theology is currently being taught in Ireland today is how to survive without any form of state support and funding. The cost of delivering education programmes in Ireland has increased enormously over the last number of years; at the same time, investments and endowments, upon which many private colleges depend, are declining in value, or their use for new and emerging needs is legally constrained. Whereas in the past, institutes could be run and courses could be delivered by priests/religious who did not expect or demand proper remuneration, today this is no longer the case, for a number of reasons:

- priests/religious and/or the orders/congregations/dioceses to which they belong have an expectation of and need of proper remuneration.
- suitably qualified priests/religious no longer exist in sufficient numbers to staff these places.
- in any case, expertise now lies with lay people, themselves often graduates of these institutes/programmes.
- an inequitable situation has developed whereby the kind of theology being enunciated speaks of a model of collaboration between clergy and laity, while in practice governance of these institutions remains with priests/religious.

- being employed on a part-time basis only limits possibilities regarding research and publication, supervision of postgraduates etc.
- without significant funding it is impossible to develop proper theological resources, fund research projects, provide for sabbaticals, etc.

Where theology is part of a state-funded institution for the most part it managed to get in by the backdoor. In reality, there are only a handful of lecturing posts in theology in Ireland that are properly remunerated. This is a major stumbling block for the development of the discipline of theology into the future. It means that many lay people will not be able to make a career in theology, and it would seem that there will *only* be lay people! Is this likely to change? Do we believe that in the future, new departments of theology will be developed at universities and/or existing institutes will be incorporated in to universities? I would be less than confident, at least with regard to the immediate future. Our understanding of education is changing profoundly. Distinctions such as formal/informal, fulltime/part-time and so on, are breaking down. In addition, the demographics would indicate that Ireland will probably need fewer full-time places at third level in the future. This will mean fewer full-time academic staff, and fewer still, it would seem, in Arts and the Humanities.

b) Earlier Efforts to Integrate Theology into the University
An important conference took place in University College Cork in 1995. Organised by Padraig Corkery and Fiachra Long, it had as its goal the establishment of a theology department at UCC. The papers and their subsequent publication provide an important historical record of the efforts in this country to get theology established within the

university, and of the perceived social and ecclesial fall-out from its absence.[7] The papers also catalogue missed opportunities by both university and ecclesiastical authorities. The issue of academic freedom was thrashed out and the merits and appropriateness of theology as opposed to Religious Studies was discussed. In this regard Seán Freyne's reflection on the Trinity College experience is particularly valuable.[8] John A. Murphy's contribution to the debate was also quite remarkable: he saw no place for theology in the university: 'I see theology *per se* as really sophisticated speculation about the unknowable ... apologetics in disguise'.[9] Murphy took the view that, as there are opportunities for worship on campus, chaplaincy services, references to religion in disciplines such as sociology, history and so on, there is little justification for theology. I remember thinking when I read this at the time that such ignorance of the true nature of theology in an eminent scholar such as John A. Murphy was itself justification for the discipline's inclusion in the university.

Today, the arguments about methodology, theology versus Religious Studies, academic freedom, and so on, are of relatively less importance. A whole new and far more pragmatic set of questions now have to be dealt with, and these pertain to the changing nature of formal education as a whole and in particular to the future of the university.

c) The University: a Changing Landscape
Most of us are aware of the crisis that is facing the Humanities in Ireland, and how changes are taking place in university that threaten to undermine if not fatally damage the place of Humanities and Liberal Arts departments in Irish universities. This crisis impinges in particular on theology as a discipline. It impacts on departments already established and it adversely affects the chances of new departments and schools

becoming established. As I said, most of our departments have got in by the backdoor, and we have never really managed to move too far away from it.

To get a sense of the direction that state-funded higher education is going in Ireland, one has only to consider recent newspaper articles by present and former members of the Conference of Heads of Irish Universities as well as by Higher Education Authority personnel. The following are some of the key points:

> Third level institutions are criticised for what is called 'mission drift'. This means, for example, that Institutes of Technology should not aspire to develop Humanities faculties; similarly Colleges of Education should confine themselves to teacher training.

Institutions are best seen as businesses. They should have 'business incubator units'. They are to see themselves as servants of enterprise and there should be much more co-operation between private industry and the university. The enterprise sector and private industry should have an increased role in the governing bodies of colleges. Over time, state control and state funding will be cut back.

The best way to achieve the desired transformation is through 'incentives'; by creating a competitive environment for funding, by tying salaries and research grants to performance indicators; and by the introduction of university league tables.

Where Arts and Humanities faculties exist, they will be valued insofar as they serve the enterprise agenda by producing graduates with a useful skills base.

These articles have been so uniform in content, and so frequent throughout 2004, that one can only assume that they are part of a deliberate campaign to direct public opinion along the lines expressed in the recent (16/9/04) 'Review of National Policies for Education: Review of Higher Education in Ireland' conducted by the OECD. The intention is that in the future, Irish education will resemble Los Angeles more than Leuven, the University of Texas more than that of Tübingen. Therefore it is worth paying some attention to what American intellectuals are saying about the changing landscape of American universities. Frank Rhodes, President Emeritus of Cornell University, can bring our reflections here one step further:

> The centuries old monopoly on education enjoyed by the universities is over, a casualty to new means of learning (information technology [IT] and the Internet) and new providers (especially corporate vendors and for-profit vendors). The universities once controlled access to knowledge, represented by both their vast libraries and the professional skills and expertise of their faculties. They controlled accreditation, graduation, and certification, and they controlled the place, time, style and substance of learning. No more. The traditional pattern of learning – by college-age students enrolled on a full-time basis in a residential, rigidly sequential program – is already being replaced by on-demand, anytime, and often on-line learning from an increasingly competitive 'knowledge business'. Skills are acquired as needed for changing careers and changing job demands by cost-conscious knowledge shoppers of every age.[10]

Rhodes cites Peter Drucker:

> Thirty years from now the big university campuses will be relics. Universities won't survive. It's as large a

change as when we first got the printed book...
Already, we are beginning to deliver more lectures and
classes off-campus via satellite or two-way video at a
fraction of the cost. The college won't survive as a
residential institution. Today's buildings are hopelessly
unsuited and totally unneeded... I consider the
American research university of the last 40 years to be
a failure. The great educational needs of tomorrow are
not in the research side but on the learning side.[11]

To many of us, this represents a glimpse of the apocalypse,
and perhaps academics, who think methodically and over
decades, are least suited to read what is happening.
Nonetheless, it is clear that universities will only survive by
adapting considerably, and their chances of survival will be
proportionate to their ability to deliver just-in-time knowledge,
skills on demand, and cost-effective learning which at the same
time is clearly understood to contribute to the economy,
though lip-service may continue to be paid to the idea of
universities contributing to society. At the same time we have
not even begun to register the impact of technology both on
what we understand as knowledge and how and where people
will access it.[12]

d) An Attempt at Evaluation
Where does this leave theology, and efforts to get theology
into the university? I think that our theology departments and
institutes have one distinctive advantage: we are used to
having to struggle to survive. However, I think we could lose
our 'competitive advantage' so to speak, by over-focusing on
how we get into the university or state educational system, a
system itself undergoing profound change. I am struck by the
fact that state funded universities are going to find themselves

in very similar situations to those in which private colleges currently find themselves. At the same time, private colleges that would succeed in integrating into these universities are likely to find themselves with the same problems that they have now, but with much less autonomy. Perhaps their situation will even be worse: resources, for example, valuable property, will have been 'colonised'.

In the light of all of this, the question of how theology can get into the university might be dated, and even conservative. Instead, we need to ask:

- Can universities in the future provide the kind of context required for the study of a discipline such as theology? What unique opportunities present themselves for the teaching of theology on university campuses? Are there inevitable compromises?

- What steps do we need to take to ensure that critically enquiring young people will want to take theology programmes, and how do these need to be packaged in order to facilitate access?

- How can colleges which are part of the mission of the Church best position themselves? How can the ecclesial mission of such colleges to the Irish education system be best articulated at this time? What steps need to be taken, what resources need to be garnered, to make this happen?

- Will the normalisation of life-long learning mean that more people will be interested in pursuing theology, and how can we facilitate them?

- What are the new intellectual landscapes for interaction with the emerging culture? How do we ensure that theology is present in these new contexts?

It could be that emerging higher education strategies in Ireland will eventually be recognised as defective, and in the meantime we should proceed – albeit with caution – to develop theology departments in Irish universities. At the same time we should try to anticipate what the educational landscape in Ireland will look like further down the road and position ourselves accordingly.

4. Conclusion

Theology in Ireland has been characterised by institutional homelessness. It has been homeless with regard to universities, where, with a few exceptions, it has barely managed to squat inside the door. Theology and theologians have also experienced a certain kind of homelessness with regard to the institutional Church, with the exception of seminaries in which theology became overly domesticated. I would suggest that this experience of homelessness has had the effect, until now, of keeping those involved in pastoral ministry as well as academic theologians closer together, and that the disorder and discomfort experienced by Irish theologians has not been all negative for the Church's mission.

At the same time, the situation cannot and will not go on as it has been. So as new and very welcome opportunities open up here for more structured employment of theologians in university and ecclesial settings, I would like to end by sounding what may seem like an odd note of caution. It has to do with the danger of careerism.

We can see this already in the university context. In a world in which knowledge is increasingly regarded as a commodity, students focus on what will get them a job, and staff can be tempted to focus merely on what will get them a better one. We have seen the shift away from seeing one's work as a vocation in a number of professions: teaching and nursing spring to mind. Clergy and pastoral workers are not exempt from the danger of careerism either. Significantly, Paul Zulehner has noted the emergence of a new kind of priest, conservative theologically, but very up to date in terms of his rights and responsibilities as well as his working hours. For this type of priest, particularly common among more recent recruits, *Berufung* (vocation) is less part of his identity than *Beruf* (profession).[13] This can be true of lay pastoral workers as well.

Evolving 'professionalism' and narrow careerism are to some extent an understandable reaction to experiences of exploitation in the past. However, they might also have something to do with doubts about identity and a loss of confidence in the inherent value and preciousness of our work. It is increasingly a rare privilege to be able to work at something that one enjoys and in which one believes. A fascinating study of young people, who live lives in which social engagement and voluntary commitment play a significant part, showed that religion and spirituality are key motivating factors in promoting service.[14] The ripple effect of those of us who are pastors and theologians collapsing into professionalism and narrow careerism would be felt in many other walks of life, aside from the counter-witness it would be to our work.

The memoriam card for Karl Rahner ends with the following:

> He loved the Church and his order, and he spent his life's energy in the service of the Church without allowing himself to become discouraged. What remains in the memory of those who knew him is his personal modesty, a preferential option for ordinary and poor people as well as for young people, a deep and honest faith, and a steadfast engagement in the pursuit of truth and justice.

In a collection such as this, that honours two men whose life and work were so gracefully and efficaciously a unity, we can do no better than to entrust our future to their inspiration and protection.

Notes

1   John O'Donohue, 'Theology in Ireland Today', *The Furrow*, (Dec 1991), p. 694.
2   ITA Statement, 'The Context of Theology In Ireland Today', *The Furrow*, (Dec 1991), p. 731.
3   Werner Jeanrond, 'The Agenda for Theology in Ireland Today III', *The Furrow*, (Dec 1991), p. 707.
4   See D. Vincent Twomey, *The End of Irish Catholicism?* Dublin: Veritas, 2003, p. 161.
5   'The Future of Theology,' *TI* 11, p. 145.
6   D. Vincent Twomey, *The End of Irish Catholicism?* Dublin: Veritas, 2003, p. 159.
7   Padraig Corkery and Fiachra Long, eds., *Theology in the University*, Dublin: Dominican Publications, 1997.
8   *Ibid.*, pp. 35-48.
9   *Ibid.*, p. 33.
10 Frank H. T. Rhodes, *The Role of the American University. The Creation of the Future*, Ithaca and London: Cornell University Press, 2001, p. xii.
11 Cited in Rhodes, *The Role of the American University*, p. xiii
12 See Michael Breen, Eamonn Conway and Barry McMillan, *Technology and Transcendence*, Dublin: Columba Press, 2003.
13 Paul Zulehner and Anna Hennersperger, *'Sie gehen und werden nicht matt.' Priester in heutigen Kultur*, Ostfildern: Schwabenverlag, 2001, p. 31.
14 Laurent A. Parks Daloz, Cheryl Keen, James Keen and Sharon Daloz Parks, *Common Fire: Lives of Commitment in a Complex World*, Boston: Beacon Press, 1997.

CHAPTER SIX

Theology in Ireland: Changing Contours and Contexts – A Response

—— Linda Hogan ——

We are indebted to Dr Conway for such a comprehensive analysis of what are undoubtedly some of the most significant challenges that face those of us who are interested in the complexion of as well as the fate of theology in contemporary Ireland.

One of the first things that strikes me is that many of the issues that are raised do not just pertain to theology, but to the Humanities more generally. Here I am speaking of the comments about the expectation that the market, and indeed government has, that universities will be places wherein subjects that are useful or relevant will be taught. We have not yet reached the situation in Ireland wherein a Minister for Education would describe the Arts as 'those decorative subjects' (as was the case in Britain), but I think that it is true to say that in Ireland too, the prevailing view of the nature of the university and the subjects it teaches is largely instrumentalist, and this threatens all the Arts (Humanities and Letters).

The enterprise culture and the rhetoric of the market means that many of those who shape education policy operate with a very truncated view of education and particularly of third-level education.

There are many points that are made that I would endorse wholeheartedly for instance:

- the insistence that theology is essentially an ecclesial activity.
- the comments that it does not seem to be regarded as the *essential* ecclesial activity that it is.
- the downplaying of the term 'crisis' as it pertains to theology in contemporary Ireland.
- the assertion that when we speak about theology in Ireland that we acknowledge and appreciate the fact that this reflection takes place in many diverse contexts, in new ways and by people who would not traditionally have been thus engaged.

I understand my task as respondent to be to highlight some of the issues that merit further exploration, and though there are many that I think are worth taking up, I am going to restrict myself to just two:

- What issues are raised for the ecclesia from the (correct) assertion that theology is essentially an ecclesial activity, specifically how can the diversity of theological reflection in Ireland be truly honoured; or at least how can it be protected?

and

- Given this characterisation of theology, on what basis should we expect the university, i.e. the state, to fund this 'loving reflection on the wisdom that resides in a believing community'?

1. Understanding Theology as Essentially an Ecclesial Activity

Dr Conway suggests that the migration of theology from church-controlled seminary contexts to institutions with merely formal or no ecclesiastical control raises questions about whether we understand or wish to understand theology as essentially an ecclesial activity. Moreover he mentions lots of reasons why theologians might wish to shed the ecclesial mantle — being ignored by bishops, disagreeing with doctrinal positions on moral matters, for example.

Although these developments may have the effect he suggests, I think that they point to a dissatisfaction with how the ecclesial context and mission of theology is understood, rather than a case of theologians questioning or abandoning its ecclesial nature. Now I agree that theology is essentially an ecclesial activity — I do not think it makes sense to think of it in any other terms, but I would like to suggest that in affirming this we must face the fact that there is significant tension within the church precisely related to this issue. He mentions the importance of exploring how it can be *in right relationship* with the Church/Churches as bodies, and that by *right relationship* is not meant simple submission, but does not say what this right relation might consist of.

Catholic theology today is characterised by deep divisions on a number of serious issues, and especially ecclesial ones. One of the most contentious revolves around conceptualisations of magisterial authority in relation to personal moral responsibility, and the related issue of the role of the theologian. Moreover we find it very difficult to live respectfully with the reality of differing and conflicting responses to important moral and ecclesial matters. We are living in a deeply polarised church and I am not sure that I agree with the very benign picture that is painted of the ecclesial context. Part of the reality is a context in which theology often sees itself as under threat. It is at least arguable that the relative absence of formal restrictive practices in Ireland may precisely be the result of our accepting a culture of self-censorship. I do not really want to open a debate about whether or not theologians have more or less freedom here than in other countries. However I do want to point out that whether they are or are not being given considerable freedom the context of which Dr Conway speaks is still one of magisterial control, the model of church is one in which authority is seen to reside among a particular group.

I certainly do not want to inflame what is an already difficult situation. However, I do want to suggest that it is increasingly difficult to maintain what in short hand is often called the legacy of Vatican II. That one can be a loyal and committed member of the church while at the same time dissenting on certain matters is precisely what is being contested. And of course this is not just an issue for those working in the field of theology, but also for every member of the community.

So when we speak about the importance of honouring the diversity of theology in Ireland, I think that a far more difficult and urgent task relates to *protecting* that diversity. It is precisely in hospitals, schools, prisons and development work, for instance that we come face to face with the theological issues that are most contested and for which new answers are needed. When people who have traditionally been excluded from theological reflection begin to engage in it, we cannot expect that the inherited frameworks will survive, or that they will only require minor modifications. However, I do not think that we inhabit a theological or ecclesial context in which this creativity is welcomed.

In addition to considering the ecclesial questions I think it is also worth examining at least one of the social/political aspects of this characterisation of theology.

2. Theology in the University

Specifically I want to ask are we right to expect the state to fund this 'loving reflection on the wisdom that resides in a believing community' or at least under what conditions are our expectations reasonable? Of course this is a difficult question to raise in such a gathering, and I am aware I do so as a member of one of the few schools that is very grateful to receive state-funding. My purpose in raising it, however, is really so that we can have the opportunity to articulate clearly how that ecclesial nature and purpose fits in the context of a secular institution.

Let me get one thing out of the way. Very often the choices vis-à-vis the university are presented in this way – we can choose between *either* Religious Studies (the scientific study of religion as a phenomenon, incorporating sociology, history of religions, anthropology, politics of religion etc) *or* Christian theology, with theologians usually mounting a defence of theology, though often on grounds that could apply to the importance of philosophy or to any other Humanities subject. Now though we would surely benefit in this country from having at least one university in which the scientific study of religion as a phenomenon (Religious Studies) were possible, I think that the importance of theology in the university can best be asserted or argued for if it were in a multi-religious context.

I believe that Irish society would greatly benefit if we had spaces in the universities wherein those who engage in scholarly reflection in their respective traditions could pursue their vocations. I think what we are in urgent need of are teaching and research contexts that are multi-religious:

contexts in which devotees of the various traditions, increasingly visible in our country, are supported in the critical reflection on their faith. What I have in mind is a school or schools where 'insiders' from multiple traditions are doing theology or jurisprudence or however one can best describe this critical reflection on texts, traditions and values. (I think that the choice of either Christian theology or religious studies simply misses the point.)

Rather I think that a compelling case for Christian theology in the university can be made only if Christian theologians also support other traditions in their attempts to find hospitable academic environments in which they too can engage in loving reflection on the wisdom that resides in their believing communities. The public square is one that is saturated with religious voices and not (as liberalism would have it) a religiously neutral one. However, universities have, for the most part, reflected this mistaken liberal assumption that religion is or at least should be a private matter. Thus my way of understanding why Christian theology should have a place in the modern university is by refuting the public/private dichotomy that liberalism constructs and by arguing that it is precisely in society's interest that religious traditions are supported in their self-critical reflection. Moreover it has, or should have, an interest in enabling religions to engage in multiple inter-religious dialogues.

Now of course it may be utopian to think that in a context when governments are reducing funding to third-level education that we can expect them to embrace the idea of funding an even more expensive programme. However, I think that this is precisely the kind of context in which Christian theology would flourish and I think it is in this context that one can make a compelling case for state funding.

IV.

Christian Identity in a Postmodern Age

CHAPTER SEVEN

Christian Identity in a Postmodern Age: A Perspective from Lonergan

—— Michael Paul Gallagher ——

Introduction

Nearly twenty years ago the American novelist Walker Percy offered what he called a diagnosis of the malaise of the modern and the postmodern. His language echoed his multiple identity as a medical doctor, a Catholic convert, and a distinguished imaginative writer. In his view, if modernity is edging into a different tone called postmodernity, it is because we live in a time of exhausted dreams, of failed promises and of the breakdown of 'rational humanism'. In such a moment of crumbling illusions, it is not enough for artists or thinkers to offer a 'documentation of the fragmentation'; servants of imagination, including theologians, should give us a fuller pathology, an identification of a crippling 'ontological impoverishment', in order to imagine a healing set of options for humanity. Percy saw us as suffering from a fragile sense of identity, and suggested that only when we feel the pain of our loss can we move towards a threshold of 'extraness', to an intimation of the strange gratuitiousness that is God.[1]

Within these compressed words lies, I believe, an important perspective on the postmodern moment. Our topic need not lead us into the postmodernism of the philosophers, deconstructive or otherwise. Rather it invites us to ponder a cultural postmodernity, where ideas become images and life paradigms, and where, in Zygmunt Bauman's metaphor, everything including modernity itself has become fluid. Like Walker Percy, I want to give attention here to the lived culture of postmodernity rather than to the complex intellectual debates of postmodernism. And like him, I want to suggest that this lived postmodernity has two very different faces. One I will call 'postmodernity of the street' and in terms of spiritual diagnosis it seems a powerful source of cultural desolation today. The other I will describe as a postmodern sensibility of searching, and it can be viewed as seeking to overcome the lopsidedness of modernity, and as pointing, however tentatively, to new convergences beyond all the fragmentation. These two forms will be explored later as representing, respectively, the passive rootlessness of postmodernity and its more hopeful frontiers. I am not suggesting a total absence of connection between postmodernism and postmodernity. Probably both the nihilist and the purifying strands of postmodernism trickle down from the academy to the lifestyle, but that is not our focus here.

Where does Bernard Lonergan come into all this? There have been lively exchanges between experts about his possible relationship to philosophical postmodernism, but practically no attention to what light his thought could cast on cultural postmodernity. Even though I am mainly interested in this second area, let me indicate some of the main issues in that other debate. At first sight Lonergan's whole style of thinking would appear ferociously 'modern' in the sense of systematic and rationally ordered. He has been accused of 'privileging pure reason'[2] in a way that makes his later acknowledgement of symbols and feelings seem like an afterthought. He would find, it has been said, postmodernism to be a 'contradictory mixture' of truth and falsity.[3] If he could explore some of the postmodern thinkers he might well repeat some of his more trenchant judgements concerning 'the Babel of our day' as a 'cumulative product of a series of refusals to understand,' in need of dialectical unmasking of its tactics of 'resistance to enlightenment' and awaiting a 'full solution' only in a religious light (*CWL*, 3, 267).

In a different sense Lonergan is postmodern even in his philosophical work. His great achievement in *Insight* was to overcome the epistemological distortions of modernity, ultimately in defence of faith. It is worth recalling that one of his earliest writings as a philosophy student drew inspiration from Newman in order to defend the act of judgement as the axis of a truth that is not narrowly scientific.[4] Some thirty years later *Insight* tackles the same challenge with much more sophisticated tools but proposing basically the same core position. Enlightenment modernity had muddied the waters, and by confusing or fusing interpretation with judgement had left us without a valid criterion of truth. Lonergan, through his elaborate analysis of cognitional structure and in particular by the centrality he gave to the act of affirmative judgement (his rereading of Newman's illative sense), was able to offer what Glenn Hughes and Sebastian Moore have called 'therapy for modernity'.[5] In this sense he is trans-modern, or (to cite a recent coinage) 'past-modern', if not exactly postmodern in the usual sense.

Linked with this theme is the question debated by several recent commentators whether Lonergan should be described as foundationalist or not. In one sense, obviously, yes. He would probably view the more fashionable cult of anti-foundationalism as rooted in a fear of order, a cowardice to think things through and to search out the perennial grounds of human knowing. However, the fine work of Ulf Jonsson has shown that Lonergan does not place 'his epistemic foundations in any kind of propositional elements' or some version of incorrigibility, but in the transcultural performance of judgement.[6]

Any summary of the *status questionis* on Lonergan and postmodernism must acknowledge some important articles by Fred Lawrence on this theme. In 2002 he summed up his position in these words: 'Lonergan's life was dedicated to helping Christian theology make the transition to what is now being called "postmodernity" without losing its integrity. His key critique of "classicism" and nuanced acceptance of "historical mindedness" is a balanced yet radically postmodern critique of modernity.'[7] Two years earlier he had written that 'Christian philosophy and theology today have something important to learn from postmodernism' and 'Lonergan can help us to learn it' through his exploration of 'the grounds of intellectual honesty'.[8] In particular he shows that 'contingency is compatible with intelligibility and truth'[9] and is able to take 'relativity seriously without being relativistic'.[10] In this context Lawrence interpreted Lonergan as sharing the 'second thoughts' of postmodern thinkers about two key developments within modernity – Enlightenment rationality and the Romantic reaction to it. This is also where intellectual history flows into what I am calling 'cultural postmodernity,' because these two streams – of 'utilitarian' and 'expressive individualism' – continue, in Lawrence's words, to 'dominate the cultural climate today'.[11] What is Lonergan's response to the inherited culture of the merely autonomous self? We glimpse an answer in a final point from Fred Lawrence: he sees Lonergan's analysis of transcendence, crowned in the transformative gift of religious love, as a 'radical dismantling of the modern subject', as a postmodern decentering or displacement of a specifically Christian kind.[12]

1. Discernment of Pluralism

Postmodern culture, both philosophical and of the street, rightly recognises a plurality of cultures, but then tends to jump to the conclusion that every culture is equally valid, and that it is totalitarian to suggest any evaluation of cultures from the outside. Such an ideological pluralism would abdicate any possibility of discernment of culture from a religious point of view. Although Lonergan gave more attention to doctrinal than to cultural pluralism, what he offers can help us distinguish between genuine pluralism and its potential slide into relativism. With typical precision Lonergan identifies 'three sources of pluralism': cultural differences that 'give rise to different brands of common sense'; the clash between differentiated and undifferentiated consciousness; the presence or absence of one or more of three forms of conversion, intellectual, moral and religious (*Method*, 326). This is not the place to expand on these fruitful pointers.[13] Suffice it to recall two of Lonergan's warnings on this topic. In 1971 he argued that the dominant philosophies of the last few centuries 'can prove a trap that confines one in a subjectivism and a relativism' (*CWL*, 17, 88). In 1982 he added that unless theologians are themselves involved in the adventure of their own conversion, 'they will be countenancing a greater pluralism than can be tolerated' (*3C*, 248). Clearly these evaluations of pluralism are still of considerable relevance for the struggle against relativism, both theoretical and lived, a delicate topic that remains central in theology's encounter with the postmodern.

Pluralism is not just an intellectual challenge. Postmodernity means living with explosive complexity, with the plurality of images all around us. The psychologist Robert Kegan sees the postmodern not so much as a 'different way of thinking' but rather as a transformation of our consciousness, confronting us with a 'multiform' set of systems that few people have the equipment to grasp.[14] Perhaps what Lonergan meant by a method of interiority is precisely the answer – a leap of quality in self-presence to one's own operations, as a foundation for consolation amid complexity. In Anne Hunt's words, 'a newly differentiated consciousness is required to meet the contemporary need for meaning'.[15]

Leaving Lonergan aside for the moment, what is implied by the question of identity in a postmodern sociocultural context? I want to evoke first the negative side of postmodernity of the street, which I will accuse of fomenting cultural desolation. More than thirty years ago Jean Baudrillard spoke of a ghost of fragility haunting an aimless culture of affluence.[16] A vulnerable sense of identity seems to be one of the characteristics of our time and often this is described in negative terms such as fragmentation, boredom, 'depthless' floating (Hans Bertens), indifference, indeterminacy, multiple selves, passivity, a retreat to the private cocoon. Where pluralist images dominate everyday culture, they serve as 'disembedding mechanisms' and 'produce a paralysis of the will'.[17] This is a heavy and heady analysis but alas there is frail human reality behind the jargon.

2. Three wounds of lived postmodernity
It is tempting, especially in Church circles, to lament this situation with a litany of '-isms': relativism, narcissism, hedonism, materialism, nihilism. What I am pointing to is a painful cultural condition where these '-isms' are more lived images than ideas. Indeed I would argue that this postmodernity of the street wounds people in three crucial

dimensions of their humanity of particular importance for religious identity: a wounded imagination, a wounded memory, and a wounded sense of belonging. The imagination, which according to Newman is the highroad of faith, can become colonised by junk food and shrink into superficiality. The memory, which is the receiver of the word through a living tradition, simply loses its powers and 'alienated immediacy' takes over. Belonging with others in some kind of cohesive community is undermined when complexity reigns, when anchors are lost and when an imposed loneliness goes hand in hand with a frenetic life-style. Even to talk like this can be unworthy of the real numbness of vision and horizon that this version of postmodernity can provoke. That is why I think the expression 'cultural desolation' a fruitful one. Desolation, in its spiritual sense, involves a dangerous and impotent restlessness. When it becomes a cultural paradigm, it can kill the roots of imagination, memory and relationship, and thus make Christian faith not so much incredible as unreal and unreachable. Johann Metz has offered a severe analysis of what he calls 'the widespread postmodernism of our hearts'.[18] This, in his reading, is not a matter of ideas but of a lifestyle that causes a new form of secularisation; due to a massive loss of perception our potential for compassion over suffering is dulled and hence the avenues to faith become blocked. In this perspective the lived culture can be the product and victim of what Lonergan would call threefold bias, which ranges from individual closure and laziness to the 'securer egoism of groups' in society, and finally to the entrenched pragmatism or 'overconfident shortsightedness' of the dominant culture. (3C, 31).

What else might Lonergan say about this scene which was already discernible in his day? 'Human acts,' he said in 1964, 'occur in sociocultural contexts' but the fullness of our freedom may be undermined in a herd-like culture of drifters. The drifter is 'content to do what everyone else is doing ... and the others too are apt to be drifters, each of them doing and choosing and thinking and saying what others happen to be doing, choosing, thinking, saying.' (*CWL*, 4, 224-225) Forty years on, these words seem sadly accurate as a description of the lostness characteristic of postmodernity of the street.

3. Positive or Ambiguous Convergences?

It is commonplace to speak of our culture as post-secular, post-materialist even in the same breath as we speak of it as post-Christian. If such labels are questionable, they indicate a development to be taken seriously. Some of the sociologists who wrote twenty or more years ago about irreversible secularisation are now writing about the return of religion. But of what kind of religion? About ten years ago *New Yorker* magazine had a brilliantly simple cartoon of someone at an information desk of a bookshop and the answer of the person behind the computer was: 'The Bible, that would be under self-help.' Nicholas Lash has eloquently voiced his suspicion about what passes for spirituality in the postmodern context: 'it does not stretch the mind or challenge our behaviour. It tends to soothe rather than subvert out well-heeled complacency.'[19]

If such fashions are escapist and ambiguous, that is not the whole story. There seems to be a genuine hunger for something beyond ourselves, a hunger that is less hidden or silent than a generation back. Perhaps our best guide is David Tracy, himself a student of Lonergan. In recent years he has argued that postmodernity is both a cultural and religious phenomenon inviting us towards healing convergences: here the courage and cost of prophetic commitment can meet the mystical sense of God's silence. In his view the postmodern religious sensibility is retrieving a sense of God at the same time 'relational', 'ethical-political', 'prophetic' and 'disruptive.'[20] A similarly positive reading of postmodernity is offered by Elizabeth Johnson who sees it as bringing together a sense of humble fragility, connectedness and a revaluing of community.[21]

This postmodernity, marked by a new openness towards the spiritual, represents a different cultural sensibility that should not be dismissed even if it sometimes seems to satisfy itself with sub-Christian answers. The full answer, and one that could nourish Christian identity today, is not spirituality on its own. If the problem is cultural the answer cannot be merely personal. If the crisis stems from a shared lifestyle, a merely individual spirituality is not enough. And so what Lonergan recognised as the positive emerging consciousness concerning religious experience has to be linked with what he stressed on many occasions – the witness of a community that makes its 'common meaning' constitutive by incarnating it in definite practices (*Method*, 358). In this sense he also spoke of theology as praxis (*3C*, 196).

4. The Retrieval of Religious Experience

To the best of my knowledge, Lonergan never explicitly tackled the idea of the postmodern. But what we have described here as a new frontier is surely in tune with his crucial retrieval of religious experience as the affective and effective source of religious conversion. As distinct from *Insight* which, on his own admission, paid no attention to the subject's religious horizon in its discussion of God's reality, after 1965 for Lonergan the God question 'arises out of religious experience' (*CWL*, 17, 208). We are loved into love by the surprise of God's love poured out, and this spiritual event is given a foundational role in doing empirical theology for today. This process which begins in affectivity and ultimately draws us into realms of unknowing seems to pre-echo, so to speak, the postmodern attention to layers of consciousness that explode beyond the merely rational. In Denise Carmody's words the religious experience explored by the later Lonergan occurs 'in a world of immediacy where image, symbol, language, [and] doctrine' lose their relevance.[22] Does this mean that we lose our Christian identity in a vague convergence of transcultural unity? By no means. In Lonergan's words the 'religious experience of the Christian is specifically distinct from religious experience in general. It's intersubjective. It's not only this gift of God's love, but it has an objective manifestation of God's love in Jesus Christ' (CWL, 17, 218).

The distinction and yet connection between a transcultural experience of the Spirit and a more definitely Christian identity is an area of which Lonergan became increasingly aware. In an unusual, if somewhat uneven, paper of 1975 he explored new convergences of an inter-religious kind. Here he drew on Fred Lawrence's notion of a 'second enlightenment', applying it interestingly to 'emerging religious consciousness' (3C, 63-65). He offered examples of reversals of the assumptions of modernity, starting from the sciences: the 'deductivist world of mechanist determinism' was being replaced by 'probability schedules of a world in process' (3C, 64). Similarly in philosophy the rationalism of the earlier enlightenment gave way to an explosion of interest in the drama of human freedom, as found in such various thinkers as Kierkegaard, Nietzsche, and Blondel. Describing this second enlightenment as a 'culturally significant' transformation (3C, 65), he went on to suggest parallels in the religious field. Bringing together such writers as Raimundo Panikkar, Teilhard de Chardin and William Johnston, he diagnosed a key distortion in modernity in 'the isolated individualism of misconceived freedom' (3C, 66) and a contrary contemporary quest for retrieving the common factor of spiritual experience in all religions. This shared foundation according to Lonergan can be found in the 'infrastructure' of religious experience prior to credal formulations. In Christian terms this infrastructure is the gift of God's love from the Spirit. But 'the distinctiveness of Christianity' (3C, 71) lies more in its superstructure, in other words, in its founding events and narratives, in the incarnation, death and Resurrection of Christ, and all that they come to mean in the life practices and commitments of the Church.

5. Differentness of Christian Identity

It is not, however, in the universal gift of God that we find our full Christian identity. It is right to recognise that the second enlightenment values the common experiential ground between religious traditions. But the syncretist side of such emerging consciousness wants to search no further, and hence is in danger of relativism and of a failure of religious imagination (to use a term from Newman). Christian identity, especially in a postmodern moment of fragmentation and pluralism, needs the courage to be 'distinctive.' It also needs to go beyond the trap of what he called 'isolated individualism', which, as already mentioned, can be found in subtle ways even in Catholic spirituality today. If Christian identity means living out the differentness of Christ, it cannot be a merely individual matter. In a postmodern context, with all its pressures and complexities, it is understandable to look to spirituality as a source of nourishment, as a key road towards mature faith and hence towards living out a Christian identity. But what kind of spirituality? If it means only inner exploring, even with a Christ focus, it may not meet the challenge of our time.

The identity challenge is cultural and so the answer has to be communal and cultural, not just individual and inner. As Lonergan once said we have not so much a crisis of faith as of culture. I would link that with a claim much repeated by Pope John Paul II: a faith that does not become culture has not been fully lived. In this light we cannot build Christian identity for today through spiritual journeys that ignore the conflicts of culture, the call to discern, transform and recreate culture, both high and ordinary. A tall order, but it is the drama of the gospel in history now as always. Here I reach for three authors that Lonergan could not have known and for answers that go beyond his explicit statements. In a book which appeared in 2002 Jean-Louis Souletie explored three models of nourishing Christian identity for today: the dialectical, the correlational and the prophetic.[23] The dialectical stresses the Word of God as interruption into history and as a challenge to take a stand. Hence Christian identity is seen as radically different to any worldly wisdom. The correlational sees grace in ordinary and non-religious spheres, stressing that our avenues to God lie within our desires, options and deepest experiences. Here Christian identity is more anthropological, more a question of the fullness of life. There are valid strengths in both schools of thought, but Souletie argues that for this postmodern moment an alert prophetic proposition of meaning is what is most needed. This requires a coherent witness through the lifestyle and practices of the Christian community. It needs to model a counter-cultural praxis, in a liberating rather than in a negative tone. Hence Christian identity would draw on all its spiritual resources and forms of wisdom to offer to the postmodern world a living reminder of a meaning received in Christ and liveable fruitfully even today. I think Lonergan would find himself in basic agreement with Souletie in this emphasis on prophetic community mission, even if his own horizons were much more wide ranging.

Secondly I want to mention an article by José Reding of Louvain, where he talks of the 'exculturation' of religion in Western Europe (a term from Danièle Hervieu-Léger's book on the end of the Catholic world in France). In Reding's view faith has less and less cultural presence in Europe, as the latest wave of secularisation invades even the private sphere of imagination. Hence he would criticise the whole concept of Christian identity as in danger of nostalgia, unless it can speak to the postmodern sensibility which hinges on individual freedom to enjoy existence. A new Christian identity, he suggests, would retrieve the gospel gateways of a different joy and a different freedom, would witness in silence rather than with explanatory words, would create a fragile visibility from below rather than dream of a pre-modern institutional identity from above.[24] One can recall Lonergan's words of 1965 warning against a false conservatism 'determined to live in a world that no longer exists' but also against a confused left wing chasing every 'new possibility' (C, 267). We can be so overwhelmed by the surrounding secular ocean that we risk losing our anchors.

More ambitious and wide-ranging is the theology of Pierangelo Sequeri, the Milan-based theologian who offers a subtle discernment of the temptations and positive potentials of postmodernity.[25] Side by side with a Metz-like critique of self-fulfilment posing as spiritual salvation (which he sees as inherited from the softer side of Romanticism), he wants to take seriously the structure of our affectivity as crucial for

Christian identity within the culture of today. Older theologies were too fixated on answering the Enlightenment on its own terms. Now we need a different 'spiritual quality' in our thinking about faith: we need to be intelligent, as always, but to broaden the agenda to include art, feelings, desires, religious experience as essential strands towards the *recognition* (a keyword) of a 'trustworthy God'. Sequeri, independently of Lonergan, talks about a retrieval of interiority, a non-romantic appraisal of falling-in-love, and a critical phenomenology of religion as key issues for faith formation in today's context.

We are reminded once again that in theology today there are many polarities. Concerning Christian identity in a postmodern culture there is tension between an emphasis on continuity, dialogue and listening to the culture on the one hand and an emphasis on discontinuity, proclamation and critique of the culture on the other hand. One school feels the need to stress Christian differentness and to establish boundaries, the other seeks out analogies and relationships in a spirit of 'expanding boundaries'.[26] Lonergan would lean towards the mediation school but he would also want to discern and judge the culture, especially where the dominant culture can be a dehumanising source of contagious decline and of 'the trivialisation of human life in the pursuit of fun' (*Method*, 105).

To sum up: the postmodern situation is a new wavelength of culture, ambiguous and promising like everything human. In terms of Christian identity it seems more important to discern the postmodern sensibility than to remain exclusively with its philosophical aspects. In particular we are invited to be convergence thinkers, seeking to heal the divorces in our thinking and our living. We recognise convergences between religions, between our own split consciousness, between mind and spirit, between feelings and philosophies. But as a delicate discernment, we are also asked to be definitely rooted in a specific Christian identity. In gospel terms we are, as always, invited to be in the world but not of it, to be both doves and serpents in our interpretations and responses. Being a serpent means judgment, dialectic, taking a stance, the courage of critique and of self-critique. Lonergan might say that being a dove means understanding before one can judge. It is grounded in experience, it strives to interpret with compassion for the pained history of our struggling situation. A Christian identity worthy of today will not come from innocently inhaling all the polluted air around, but neither will it come from merely moaning about the dangers, or from jumping to judgement without the uphill journey of trying to understand the new scene. A Christian identity will have the imagination to be different – a postmodern keyword – but that imagination is nourished from the longer and larger story of God's entry into our adventure of meaning. To echo a gospel parable, we need to cherish our inherited roots and to develop branches that reach out and give shelter to our wounded but wondering world.

[For the abbreviated references to Lonergan's works given in parentheses in the text, see the list of Abbreviations at the beginning of the book.]

Notes

1 'Diagnosing the Modern Malaise' (1985) in Walker Percy, *Signposts in a Strange Land*, ed., Patrick Samway, New York: Noonday Press, 1992, pp. 204-221.

2 Ronald H. McKinney, 'Deconstructing Lonergan,' *International Philosophical Quarterly* 31 (1991), pp. 81-93, quotation from p. 84.

3 James L. Marsh, 'Reply to McKinney on Lonergan,' *Ibid.*, p. 103.

4 This student paper was entitled 'Science and True Judgment'. I have discussed it at some length in a section of a recent article: 'Lonergan's Newman: Appropriated Affinities', *Gregorianum* 85 (2004), pp. 735-56.

5 Glenn Hughes and Sebastian Moore, 'The Affirmation of Order: Therapy for Modernity in Bernard Lonergan's Analysis of Judgment', *Lonergan Workshop* 8 (1990), pp. 109-134.

6 Ulf Jonsson, *Foundations for Knowing God: Bernard Lonergan's Foundations for Knowledge of God and the Challenge from Antifoundationalism*, Frankfurt am Main: Peter Lang, 1999, p. 337.

7 Frederick G. Lawrence, 'Lonergan and Aquinas: the Postmodern Problematic of Theology and Ethics' in *The Ethics of Aquinas*, ed., Stephen Pope, Washington: Georgetown University Press, 2002, pp. 437-455. Quotation from p. 438.

8 Fred Lawrence, 'Lonergan, the Integral Postmodern?', *Method: Journal of Lonergan Studies* 18 (2000) pp. 95-122. Quotations from pp. 95, 114.

9 *Ibid.*, p. 116

10 Fred Lawrence, 'The Fragility of Conciousness: Lonergan and the Postmodern Concern for the Other', *Theological Studies* 54 (1993) pp. 55-93. Quotation from p. 56.

11 *Ibid.*, pp. 92-93.

12 *Ibid.*, p. 72.

13 For more detail see my article 'Inculturation Debates: the Relevance of Lonergan', *Studia Missionalia* 52 (2003), pp. 347-63.

14 Robert Kegan, *In Over Our Heads: the Mental Demands of Modern Life*, Cambridge: Harvard University Press, 1994, pp. 316, 321.

15 Anne Hunt, *The Trinity and the Paschal Mystery: A Development in Recent Catholic Theology*, Collegeville: Liturgical Press, 1997, p. 162.

16 Jean Baudrillard, *The Consumer Society* (1970), London: Sage Publications, 1998, p. 174.

17   Anthony Giddens, *Modernity and Self-Identity: Self and Society in the Late Modern Age*, Cambridge: Polity Press, 1991, p. 3

18   Johann Baptist Metz, *A Passion for God: The Mystical-Political Dimension of Christianity*, New York: Paulist Press, 1998, p. 28.

19   Nicholas Lash, *The Beginning and the End of 'Religion'*, Cambridge: Cambridge University Press, 1996, p. 174.

20   David Tracy, 'The Post-Modern Re-Naming of God as Incomprehensible and Hidden,' *Cross Currents* 50 (2000), pp. 240-47. Quotations from pp. 246-47.

21   Elizabeth Johnson, 'Between the Times: Religious Life and the Postmodern Experience of God', *Review for Religious* 53 (1994), pp. 6-28.

22   Denise Lardner Carmody, 'The Desire for Transcendence: Religious Conversion', in *The Desires of the Human Heart: an Introduction to the Theology of Bernard Lonergan*, ed., Vernon Gregson, New York: Paulist Press, 1988, pp. 57-73. Quotation from p. 65.

23   Jean-Louis Souletie, *La Crise: une chance pour la foi*, Paris: Editions de l'Atelier, 2002.

24   José Reding, 'Les résistances à l'évangélisation: sécularisation et mentalités nouvelles,' *Revue théologique de Louvain* 25 (2004), pp. 343-371.

25   See especially Pierangelo Sequeri, *Sensibili allo Spirito: Umanesimo religioso e ordine degli affetti*, Milan: Glossa, 2001, Chapter 1 ('La qualità spirituale nel post-moderno').

26   John D. Dadosky, 'The Dialectic of Religious Identity: Lonergan and Balthasar', *Theological Studies* 60 (1999), pp. 31-52, at p. 36.

CHAPTER EIGHT

Christian Identity in a Postmodern Age: A Perspective from Rahner

—— Declan Marmion ——

1. Religious Identity: Between Fundamentalism and Pluralism

The question of religious identity – be it Christian, Islamic or Jewish has not been far from the headlines over the last number of years. After 9/11, the terrorist attacks in Madrid, and in Russia, the debates have focused on the question of religious fundamentalism and the growing militant strain in Islam. We are experiencing a new kind of insecurity – where will the terrorists strike next? – and defensiveness. In the aftermath of the bombings in the US, sales of personal firearms and domestic security systems rocketed. In Europe too, there is a growing reaction to what is perceived as a widespread increase in religious fundamentalism. In France, for example, there has been the ban on Muslim students wearing traditional headscarves to school. While postmodern European sensibilities might tolerate religious signs and symbols that are discreet rather than overt, they are distinctly uncomfortable with overly assertive or militant forms of religious expression. The fear is that minority religious groups, who remain in self-enclosed enclaves, will not readily assimilate to the surrounding culture.

Contrasting with a sectarian understanding of religious identity is one that tries to embrace various perspectives at once – a kind of multiple religious belonging.[1] Thus, a person might claim to be part of a number of religious traditions – partly Christian and partly Buddhist, for example. Others, of course, espouse no religious affiliation and reject the absolute truth claims of all institutionalised forms of religion. So, as far as Christian tradition is concerned, there is a tension between official claims to absolute truth and uniqueness on the one hand, and an increasingly independent, sophisticated, and critical group of believers, at least in the West, on the other. The hackneyed phrase '*à la carte* Catholic' has been around for some time. Frequently employed in a derogatory sense, it represents a piecemeal approach to doctrine, practice and religious affiliation, governed primarily by personal judgement and taste. And today, this has developed into the selective appropriation of elements and beliefs of other religions and worldviews.

Where does Rahner fit into all of this and does he have anything to say to the challenges now facing us? Certainly, he acknowledged the developing religious pluralism in his time and encouraged engagement with people of other faiths. Speaking over thirty years ago he could say:

> The society in which the Catholic Christian of today lives is a complex and heterogeneous one. He or she lives in the closest proximity to, and has the closest personal connections with, non-Catholic Christians. The sphere in which one's life is passed is no longer a country which in its social, cultural and even civic aspects, is homogeneously 'Catholic'. Indeed, where formerly the individual nations were independent of one another in their lines of historical development,

nowadays these lines are tending to become fused into a single great world history. And the result of this is that the non-Christian religions and philosophies of life such as Islam, Hinduism and Buddhism, no longer constitute an area of foreign folklore which has no bearing upon the course of life modern man maps out for himself and raises no radical problems for him. Instead of this, these non-Christian religions have come to be regarded as the philosophies of life of people who have become neighbours to modern man and woman, people in whom one cannot fail to recognize just as high a degree of intelligence as that with which one credits oneself.[2]

While Rahner would not have heard of the term globalisation (he uses the term 'single great world history'), he anticipated much of the current discussion in philosophy and theology about inter-religious dialogue, pluralism and the encounter with the other. He distanced himself from exclusivist theologies that barred non-Christians from salvation. His controversial term 'anonymous Christian' allowed Christians to affirm the goodness of diverse religious traditions. Non-Christians, he maintained, can fulfil their human nature through the acceptance of God's offer of transcendence while remaining unaware of its source. While terms such as 'anonymous Christian' or 'anonymous Buddhist' might be criticised today for their self-referential constructions of otherness – they blur the distinctiveness of the other and so tend to erase the very real differences between the religions – Rahner's project has endured because he tried to maintain two essential teachings: God's universal salvific will and the christological affirmation of Jesus' role as mediator of that salvation. It was these two doctrines that would form the cornerstone of Vatican II's Declaration on Non-Christian Religions, *Nostra Aetate*.

2. Christian Identity: Negotiating the Tensions

For a good part of his life, Rahner worked against a backdrop of change in the Church. Vatican II was the benchmark here, and he strove to promote its reception whenever and wherever possible. Rahner saw the Council as a watershed marking the transition from a European and western-Church to a world-Church. Moreover, Vatican II wished to speak in a different idiom, moving away from a traditionally defensive neo-scholastic theology, towards a more missionary style aiming to speak to those for whom Christianity had become alien. This led to a positive appraisal of the great world religions and a stress on the universal and effective saving will of God. Such optimism about salvation – a theme dear to Rahner – meant that even those who seek the unknown God in shadows and images are not far from the true God, who wills all to be saved.[3]

Rahner thus anticipated many of the tensions or frictions facing Christians in an increasingly pluralistic and fragmented society. While much of his writing focused on the intra-ecclesial sphere and the need for structural change in the Church,[4] he still had to negotiate his way through various polarities. Thus we have his plea for a better balance between the authority of the magisterium, on the one hand, and the hierarchy of truths and legitimate academic freedom, on the other. Other tensions included attempting to reconcile the universality of salvation with the particularity of the Christ event, and, in a similar vein, the relationship between anonymous and explicit Christianity. Throughout such reflections, Rahner points to the transcendent nature of the human spirit, to the human person, who, by virtue of his or her dynamism and transcendent orientation, is referred to God in every act of knowledge and love. Not that Rahner's project is a thoroughgoing anthropocentric one – it is not simply the human quest for meaning and fulfilment that culminates in God. It is God who seeks out humankind with the offer of grace – a grace that is not limited to the confines of an ecclesiastical institution, but is universal.

Thus it is simplistic to pigeon-hole Rahner as belonging to a 'liberal' or 'progressive' camp. His understanding of Christian identity is more subtle than this. Steeped in the Christian tradition and the teachings of the early Church, he used these as a resource for renewing the present. One example is his work on the history and theology of penance where he retrieved a number of 'forgotten truths' concerning the practice of the sacrament over the centuries (for example, the variety of sacramental practice) that were they appropriated, might help the sacrament out of its current demise.[5] In the light of Vatican II, Rahner increasingly turned his energies to structural, spiritual and theological renewal in the Church. For him faith and religion must come from a person's 'proper and free conviction' and be capable of being experienced. Faith 'implies an existentiell, practical, and theoretical relationship to the truth of faith itself ... [and] may not be reduced to mere obedience to the formal teaching authority of the Church'.[6] Here we see the tension or friction between the authority of personal experience as a locus for grace, on the one hand, and Rahner's conviction that authentic Christianity is bound up with community and society, on the other:

> Christianity is a historical religion bound up with one Jesus Christ. I heard of him only through the Church and not otherwise. Hence I cannot be content with a

purely private Christianity which would repudiate its origins.[7]

In one sense Rahner is a child of Enlightenment modernity with its rationalistic and anthropocentric focus. But he also stresses the interdependent, other-oriented aspect of the human person: 'The free subject, even as free subject, is not absolutely self-sufficient.'[8] 'Christianity means Church ... [even if] there will always be the permanent tension, which constantly takes different forms and must always be resolved afresh, between Christian freedom and the Christian need for the Church.'[9] Thus, Rahner continually tried to find a *via media* between the institutional and the charismatic dimensions of the Church, between ecclesial authority and the freedom of the individual.[10] Towards the end of his life, however, he grew increasingly pessimistic with what he perceived as a growing restorationist mentality within the Catholic Church. Consequently, he argued for a more authentic interpretation of the Council – one, he believed, that was suggested by the Council itself.

Much discussion of the relationship between authority and freedom, tradition and recontextualisation is reflected in Rahner's own grappling with such issues. Writing in 1968, Hans Urs von Balthasar recognised as much:

Today, Rahner seems to stand undecided at a crossroads: his thoroughly Catholic heart wants him to be faithful to the visible, official and sacramental Church, but his speculative bent demands the relativisation of everything ecclesiastical in the name of an all-pervading grace.[11]

Such tensions are now more apparent than ever. Disaffection with all kinds of institutions abounds; the Churches are not unique in this. At the same time the widespread interest in spirituality reflects the need to find ways of coping with the frenzied pace of modern living and the shallowness of a competitive and materialistic culture. So, while ecclesiastical leaders bemoan the absence of reference to God in the European constitution, and see in this the loss of a Christian memory and an attempt to promote a vision of humanity without reference to our Christian roots, there is at the same time a genuine yearning for the spiritual, for some form of abiding meaning and fulfilment in lives that may be prosperous but are otherwise empty.[12]

While this situation is at a remove from the context of Rahner's theology, neither is it totally alien to him. He wrote against a backdrop of growing unbelief and indifference towards religion and for an audience that was among the most affluent in Europe. His approach in such a context was to move from a conceptual indoctrination 'from without', where the focus was on the so-called 'proofs' of God's existence and learning the propositions of faith, to a mystagogical initiation into Christianity.[13] By mystagogy, a term he derives from Maximus the Confessor (d. 662) among others, he means an initiation into the sacred, to the experience of mystery. The mystagogical approach, which is a counterbalance to an exclusively doctrinal catechesis, makes use of a whole variety of ways in which we perceive and communicate, including seeing, feeling, and hearing, and is evident in initiatives such as the RCIA and others. This mystagogical emphasis points also to Rahner's deep knowledge of the Christian tradition enabling him to draw on the riches of its spiritual heritage.

Rahner also became increasingly aware of the pluralism in human knowledge, of what he called 'gnoseological concupiscence'. Intellectually, and not only existentially, we are pulled in various directions. The multiplicity of world views and claims to truth cannot simply be harmonised or brought together. He describes the impossibility of bringing the various branches of knowledge into some form of harmonious or comprehensive view and how we are increasingly overwhelmed with information and knowledge. And Rahner was writing *prior* to our digital era! The 'interdisciplinary fragmentation' evident within his own discipline of theology meant that students starting out found it almost impossible to acquire any overarching synthesis or view of the whole.[14] Speaking in the early seventies, Rahner was already opining:

> When I began my theological studies forty years ago, I was far cleverer than I am today, if I take all the possible branches of knowledge and intellectual problems as my criterion of measurement. For today there is such a vast number of questions and areas of knowledge of a historical, metaphysical, philosophical, linguistic, sociological and religious kind that in the face of this mass of theological material I feel much stupider than I did then.[15]

Accordingly, Rahner's theological method focuses on the essentials of faith concentrating the plurality into a very few basic thoughts or key terms, of which the most basic is the experience of the self-communication of God. Like Aquinas, Rahner 'always thinks on the basis of the whole and in relation to the whole'.[16]

3. Criticisms of Rahner
The tensions in Rahner's theology and in his understanding of what it means to be a Christian are also reflected in criticisms of his work. Thus, it is not surprising that he was criticized

from both the right and from the left, for being either too radical, or not radical enough.[17] Catholic traditionalists complained that Rahner, especially since Vatican II, had relativised the radical demands of Christianity. The specificity of Christian revelation and its truth claims are jeopardized, they feel, in a too eager attempt to accommodate to the increasingly pluralistic societies of the (so-called) first world.[18]

In place of polemic, however, it is preferable to tackle these issues *with* Rahner rather than against him, in other words, to draw from within Rahner's own writings resources to respond to the various criticisms made of him. It is not that Rahner's theology represents some kind of closed 'system' – he never thought of his work in such a way.[19] Indeed, he acknowledged both the limitations of his theology as well as the need for other thinkers to develop his ideas in new directions. The whole of reality may be a harmonious symphony for Balthasar, but it is not so for Rahner.

Such criticisms of Rahner need to be viewed against the backdrop of the reception of Vatican II. There are those who feel Vatican II went too far, was too progressive and surrendered too much of the tradition for the sake of modernity. Others feel the full implications of the theology of the Council have still to be worked out, and in the light of recent restorationist tendencies are calling for a Vatican III. One's appreciation or otherwise of Rahner's theology is, therefore, directly related to how one interprets the Council and its aftermath. A perceptive commentator on Rahner, Francis Fiorenza, has put it well:

At the time of the Second Vatican Council, Rahner's method was welcomed precisely because of its anthropological starting-point and its endeavour to bring Thomist philosophy into dialogue with modern philosophy. Rahner's theology of freedom and his advocacy of free speech within the church were seen as opening the windows of the church to let in the fresh air of modernity. Today, however, his method is challenged on these very points. His anthropological starting-point is criticised as a reductive anthropocentrism, his advocacy of freedom is denounced for mirroring the self-centred autonomy of the Enlightenment, and his existential orientation is attacked as a privatising of religion that lacks social and political force.[20]

Such tensions are evident in various contemporary forms of Christian self-understanding. Some feel a more militant Christianity with a strong proselytizing thrust is called for in a hostile and de-Christianised culture. The danger however with this kind of muscular or Pelagian Christianity is that a kind of sectarianism develops, one that eschews dialogue with those of other views (other than trying to convert them). It can also lead to a ghettoisation of Christianity, the development of sect-like characteristics, and an élitist outlook. Moreover, where an overly docile attitude to authority exists, critical approaches to Christian tradition tend to be viewed as acts of disloyalty to the Church.

Rahner, for his part, might initially appear to be supporting such a view of the Church of the future when he talks about the future 'diaspora' Church of the 'little flock'.[21] By 'little flock' however, Rahner did not mean a petty sectarian mentality as a way of protecting a cosy traditionalism. If we view his ecclesiology in connection with the renewal inaugurated by Vatican II and its openness to the world, it is clear that he did not want the particularity of

Christian identity to be purchased at the price of the public character of theology. Most of his publications from the sixties onwards were of an 'ad hoc' nature – responding to particular issues of the times. He did not recommend Christians to isolate themselves from their cultural environment. In fact, as I noted earlier, he often presented the dividing line between Christians and non-Christians in a rather fluid manner. Christian identity into the future cannot be a black and white choice between a strategy of accommodation to secular thought and culture, or a kind of resistant sectarianism.

4. Christian Identity into the Future

What might a Rahner-inspired understanding of Christian identity look like? In an article entitled 'The Spirituality of the Church of the Future' (1977),[22] Rahner brought together a number of points which he considered essential to a Christian spirituality of the future. Spirituality, for Rahner, is essentially the practice of faith or lived Christianity.

His first point is that any future spirituality must preserve an element of *continuity* with the spirituality of the history of the church. Consequently, spirituality will be more than humanism. It will always be a spirituality of adoration of the incomprehensible God, find historical expression in Christian discipleship, and be lived ecclesially. Such ecclesial spirituality is rooted in a common faith, is sacramentally realised, and at the same time will have patience with those negative aspects of church life which can be a burden to one's spirituality. The challenge, then, as Rahner sees it, is for Christians to learn both positively and negatively from the Church's past: to be lovingly immersed in its spiritual heritage, while also remaining open for new beginnings emerging 'from below' inspired by the Spirit.

A second point is that spirituality should concentrate on what is *most essential* and decisive for Christian faith. Rahner is not disparaging various types of liturgical and other devotions, but he believed that spirituality in the future will concentrate on what is most essential, namely on the experience of God's self-communication to humankind. It is the experience of God which for him comprises the real basic phenomenon of spirituality. This is the assumption behind his oft-quoted phrase that the Christian of the future will be a mystic or he or she will not exist.[23] The former external or societal supports for living Christian faith are diminishing and the Christian of the future will need to have the spiritual resources to live 'from within'. Such a personal experience of God involves a decision of faith on the part of each individual, a decision sometimes of solitary courage and responsibility.

Thirdly, this experience is not confined to the extraordinary lives of the mystics and the saints – Rahner was never élitist – but penetrates every aspect of daily life through the discovery of God in all things (*das Gottfinden in allen Dingen*).[24]

Finally, his understanding of spirituality and mysticism is not that of a pure interiority divorced from the world. On the contrary, the spirituality of the future will have an explicit practical and political dimension, acknowledging its this-worldly responsibility, while also being a spirituality of hope, awaiting an absolute future and not placing its hope in an earthly utopia. Rahner increasingly saw practical theology as the critical conscience of the other theological disciplines[25] and wrote on political topics from the holocaust to nuclear warfare.

I have highlighted the centrality of spiritual experience in Rahner's thought and his belief that the personal self-communication of God was not something scarce – restricted to a privileged few, but was at the core of what it means to be Christian. True, one could question today whether he has taken sufficient account of the great diversity or plurality of religious experiences, including those of non-Christians, or whether he is simply assuming a common core to all religious experiences.[26] Nevertheless, his work has led theology to a growing rapprochement with spirituality and to an acknowledgement that religious experience cannot be dismissed as cognitively empty. In more traditional terms, theology both grows out of the spiritual life and remains in debt to it. In effect, for Rahner, this meant that non-theologians (or so-called ordinary Christians) would 'call into question the traditional theological enterprise [and] the whole way in which theologians think and reason'.[27] Rahner challenges us to a 'faith between rationality and emotion', as the title of one of his articles puts it.[28] It is not a question of theology *or* spirituality, faith *or* reason; Rahner was able to combine an attitude of relentless critical questioning alongside a life of prayer and Christian commitment.

Though Rahner's critics may have accused his theology (and also Vatican II) as overly accommodating to the surrounding culture, it would be fairer to say that he was trying to work out the full implications of his convictions about the universality of grace. In the neo-scholastic world in which Rahner began his theological training, grace was seen as scarce, restricted to the ecclesial sphere, and particularly the sacraments. It was this narrow, two-tiered, and rather dualistic framework that Rahner and others challenged. Though many of the dualisms that have bedevilled theology – between sacred and profane, the bodily and the spiritual, the self and the other – are still with us, it is to Rahner's credit that he sought a more 'holistic', if one might use that word, vision of Christianity, a vision that was ultimately more optimistic and hopeful to a post-Vatican II generation.

So, as we struggle to articulate what it means to be Christian in a postmodern, and increasingly sophisticated and pluralist society, we can still be guided by Rahner. He encourages us to move beyond a more and more vehement assertion of the truth claims of Christianity to an engagement with postmodern sensibilities. Such sensibilities recognise truth only relative to the community in which a person participate – an approach not far removed from Rahner's *Denkstil*. One of Rahner's most important contributions has been to help theology come to terms with the situated, partial and fragile character of all human knowing and doing.[29] In a postmodern vein he was aware that language has a life of its own, is open to ever-new interpretations, and so 'he is cautious about emphasising too strongly the ability of language to express matters so definitively.'[30] All faith formulations, he maintained, are ultimately relativised in the face of Holy Mystery that is their source and goal.

Rahner therefore took seriously the pluralistic, contextual and interdisciplinary[31] dimensions of Christian identity. It is not a question of ceasing to make any truth claims at all. Rather, the challenge is to bring the wisdom of Christianity and its tradition into dialogue with the longings and the searching of contemporary men and women. This calls for a love of the Church, a deep knowledge of its tradition as well as a willingness to critically reflect on how best to mediate such a rich resource today. This was Rahner's life-long project; it is still worthy of our best efforts.[32]

Notes

1   Catherine Cornille, ed., *Many Mansions?: Multiple Religious Belonging and Christian Identity*, New York: Orbis, 2002, p. 3.

2   'Church, Churches and Religions', *TI* 10, p. 30 (translation emended). See also J. Fletcher Hill, 'Rahner and Religious Diversity,' in Declan Marmion & Mary E. Hines, eds., *The Cambridge Companion to Karl Rahner* (Cambridge: Cambridge University Press, 2005), pp. 235-48.

3   'The Abiding Significance of Vatican II,' *TI* 20, p. 100.

4   Karl Rahner, *The Shape of the Church to Come*, trans. Edward Quinn (London: SPCK, 1974).

5   'Forgotten Truths Concerning the Sacrament of Penance', *TI* 2, pp. 135-74.

6   'Authority', *TI* 23, p. 84.

7   'Courage for an Ecclesial Christianity', *TI* 20, p. 9. This question is also at the heart of theological reflection on the so-called New Age spiritual movements: the exaltation of personal inner experience and a radical break with Christian tradition. See the Pontifical Councils for Culture and Interreligious Dialogue, 'Jesus Christ, The Bearer of the Water of Life: A Christian Reflection on the New Age', *Origins* 32 (2003), pp. 570-92.

8   'Authority', *TI* 23, p. 63.

9   'Why Am I a Christian Today?' *The Practice of Faith: A Handbook of Christian Spirituality*, London: SCM Press, 1985, p. 12.

10   'The Church's Responsibility for the Freedom of the Individual', *TI* 20, pp. 51-64 and 'Theology and the Roman Magisterium', *TI* 22, pp. 176-90.

11   Hans Urs von Balthasar, 'Current Trends in Catholic Theology and the Responsibility of the Christian', *Communio*, 5/1 (1978), p. 80.

12   'New Age' is the umbrella term that has been used to describe various spiritual alternatives to traditional expressions of religion. See note 7.

13   'Theological Considerations on Secularization and Atheism', *TI* 11, pp. 182-84. See also Declan Marmion, *A Spirituality of Everyday Faith: A Theological Investigation of the Notion of Spirituality of Karl Rahner*, Louvain Theological & Pastoral Monographs 23 (Leuven: Peeters Press/Eerdmans, 1998), pp. 261-80.

14   This was one of the reasons why Rahner developed an introductory course in theology aimed at providing a basic

understanding and justification of Christian faith. See *FCF*, pp. 8-14. On the question of pluralism in theology, see his, 'Pluralism in Theology and the Unity of the Creed', *TI* 11, pp. 3-23 and 'Possible Courses for the Theology of the Future', *TI* 13, pp. 32-60. The current proliferation of 'Introductions', 'Handbooks,' and 'Readers' in theology is an indication of the problem.

15   'The Foundation of Belief', *TI* 16, pp. 6-7.

16   Karl Rahner, *Everyday Faith*, London: Burns & Oates, 1967, p. 188.

17   Herbert Vorgrimler, *Understanding Karl Rahner: An Introduction to his Life and Thought*, trans. John Bowden, London: SCM, 1986, pp. 121-30.

18   A famous example of such adversarial reaction is that of Hans Urs von Balthasar in his book *Cordula oder der Ernstfall*. [ET: *The Moment of Christian Witness*, trans. Richard Beckley, San Francisco: Ignatius Press, 1969]. A second edition (1967) contained an 'Afterword' by von Balthasar as a response to the widespread criticism of his treatment of Rahner in the first edition. For a discussion of some of the issues here, see my 'Rahner and his Critics: Revisiting the Dialogue', *Irish Theological Quarterly* 68 (2003), pp. 195-212.

19   A fair evaluation of Rahner's understanding of spirituality cannot be obtained solely on the basis of a limited and arbitrary selection of his works. This is the perennial danger in any attempt to review Rahner's theology according to Johann Baptist Metz: '... and every review of his (Rahner's) theology seems almost inescapably to be in danger of roughly schematizing it or arbitrarily abridging it.' Metz, 'Foreword', *Spirit in the World*, p. xvi.

20   Francis S. Fiorenza, 'Method in Theology', in Declan Marmion and Mary E. Hines, eds., *The Cambridge Companion to Karl Rahner* (Cambridge: Cambridge University Press, 2005), pp. 65-66. Fiorenza concludes that Rahner should not be seen primarily as a philosophical epistemologist but as a practical theologian.

21   Rahner, *The Shape of the Church to Come*, pp. 29-34.

22   'The Spirituality of the Church of the Future', *TI* 20, pp. 143-53.

23   'The Spirituality of the Church of the Future', p. 149.

24   'There is a mysticism of daily living, the finding of God in all things, the sober drunkenness of the Spirit mentioned by the

Fathers of the Church and the ancient liturgy, which we dare not reject or disdain just because it is sober'. *Karl Rahner in Dialogue: Conversations and Interviews 1965-1982*, trans. Harvey Egan, New York: Crossroad, 1986, p. 297. See also Karl Rahner, *Everyday Things*, Theological Meditations 5, ed., Hans Küng, London and Melbourne: Sheed and Ward, 1965, pp. 33-41.

25   'The Future of Theology', *TI* 11, p. 134.

26   This forms part of George Lindbeck's criticism of Rahner's 'experiential-expressive' position, i.e., its espousal of a general account of human experience. See his *The Nature of Doctrine*, Philadelphia: Westminster Press, 1984, 30-45, However, I have argued elsewhere that, as far as the relationship between experience and doctrine is concerned, Rahner is more aware of its complex symbiotic and reciprocal nature than Lindbeck's account suggests. See my 'Rahner and his Critics', pp. 201-207.

27   Rahner, 'Foreword', *TI* 16, p. vii. The background for this statement was the phenomenon of the Charismatic renewal and the sceptical stance of some theologians towards it. See also his 'The Relation between Theology and Popular Religion', *TI* 22, pp. 140-47.

28   'Faith between Rationality and Emotion', *TI* 16, pp. 60-77.

29   Karl Rahner, 'Experiences of a Catholic Theologian,' trans. Declan Marmion and Gesa Thiessen, *Theological Studies* 61 (2000), pp. 3-15.

30   Craig A. Baron, 'The Poetry of Transcendental Thomism', in Lieven Boeve & John C. Ries, eds., *The Presence of Transcendence: Thinking 'Sacrament' in a Postmodern Age*, Leuven: Peeters, 2001, p. 57. Religious scholars, influenced by the writings of Derrida, Levinas, Marion and others, insist that our language about God is inadequate if not idolatrous. In thus reviving the apophatic tradition, they are also, not unlike Rahner before them, advocating a new, more tentative, way of speaking about God. See Thomas A. Carlson, *Indiscretion: Finitude and the Naming of God*, Chicago: University of Chicago Press, 1998, and John D. Caputo and Michael J. Scanlon, eds., *God, the Gift and Postmodernism*, Indianapolis: Indiana University Press, 1997.

31   Rahner was one of the first theologians to enter into dialogue with experts from other secular disciplines, including Marxists, atheists, and natural scientists. See Hans-Dieter Mutschler, ed.,

Gott neu buchstabieren. Zur Person und Theologie Karl Rahners, Würzburg: Echter, 1994, pp. 97-119.

32 I would like to acknowledge the comments and suggestions of Dr Thomas Dalzell, SM, and Dr Gesa Thiessen on an earlier version of this chapter.

V.

Spirituality and
Religious Experience

CHAPTER NINE

Attende tibi ipsi: A Note on Lonergan and Spirituality[1]

—— Hilary Mooney ——

Introduction

A first reading of the works of Bernard Lonergan can influence one for a lifetime. To borrow a metaphor from Graham Greene, it is as if one had lived 'in a wild jungle country without a map, but now the paths had been traced and naturally one had to follow them'.[2] With an author of the speculative and systematic stature of Lonergan, this path setting is particularly expansive. The orientation gained by a thorough appropriation of the structure which Lonergan identified as inherent in the conscious operations of the human subject is extensive. Lonergan's highly technical thematisation of this structure can, however, lead some of its adherents to lose a childlike wonder in the face of new ideas and hitherto uncommented phenomena. Lonergan himself was driven by an ongoing quest for *further* insight into the human subject and the world mediated by meaning in which that subject lives. Those of us who have donned the master's cloak must learn not to smother within its folds but rather to let its hem brush lightly over the contours of human living upon which our own intellectual journey invites us to reflect.

With this in mind I would like to distinguish between two ways of esteeming an author. One form of paying tribute to a respected author, is to translate all that one reads back into the terms and vocabulary of that thinker, of seeing everything through his or her glasses, judging everything to be a confirmation of his or her hermeneutic. Another form of paying tribute is, however, also possible: this involves bringing the author into a genuine dialogue with others. The testing point of the dialogue as dialogue, is the question whether these 'others' may complement his or her thought or even raise a challenge to aspects of it. At the very least an amplification of what is still implicit in the system of the prized author by means of the ideas of others ought to occur. Insofar as it is possible to distinguish these two forms of respect, I must confess, that it is my aim to pursue the second in what follows. It is an amplification of Lonergan's thought through the writings of the church fathers which I attempt here.

This dialogue with the past is undertaken on three points each of which pertains to spirituality: God and Mystery, The Human Outreach to the Divine, Knowledge Mediated through Discipleship and finally, reviewing the situation within which people in Western European countries are currently turning to God in prayer and in the life of faith. Questions raised include: What aspects of Lonergan's thought can help to make explicit the contours of a contemporary spirituality and what aspects exercise a reassuring influence on contemporary believers?

1. God and Mystery
The transcendence of God has been a matter of reflection for generations of Christian writers.[3] The human cannot comprehend the divine essence. This is not due to any

intrinsic lack of intelligibility in the divine essence; rather it is rooted in the limited capacity of the human spirit to grasp the infinite intelligibility of God. Negative theology considers the limitations of the human grasp of the divine on several levels. We may distinguish the inability to *comprehend* God, from the inability to *conceptualise* adequately that measure of knowledge which we have achieved, and further from an inability to *speak* adequately of this knowledge of God.

Now few 'negative theologies' are purely negative. A purely negative theology would be predestined to silence. One way of distinguishing between what we can know, and what we cannot know about God is the affirmation that we can only know that God exists but not what God is. This distinction goes back to the writings of the Jewish first century author, Philo of Alexandria. It also plays an important role in the writings of the fourth century Cappadocian theologian, Gregory, Bishop of Nyssa. He repeatedly emphasised that we cannot know what God's essence is; we can only know that God is. Gregory's presentation of the transcendence of God is rooted in his understanding of the divine essence as unbounded and infinite. For other authors it was not so much an ontology of the infinite God which concerned them but rather a reflection on the possibility of naming God. The most famous among the Christian negative theologians is the so-called 'Pseudo Dionysius Areopagita'.[4] In his work *De mystica theologica* he refers to an affirmative theology[5] and research has agreed that the distinction between affirmative speech about God and negative speech about God is devoted unique attention in his writings. In our affirmative speech we affirm something analogously of God, and in the negative speech we negate a predication of God. Thus we may engage in 'towards speech' about God or 'away from speech' about God.[6] We may speak of 'kataphatic' and 'apophatic' theology. Since the divine essence is always more than what can be expressed by any term, negation is the truer form of speech about God. In his third letter, the Pseudo Dionysius considers the case of the *enduring* transcendence of God in the light of the divine revelation to us in Jesus Christ. Here he claims that the mystery remains hidden both *after* the revelation of God in Jesus Christ and even *amid* this revelation.[7] Even after the incarnation, after the revelation of God in Jesus Christ, Pseudo Dionysius claims that what has been spoken remains unsaid and what has been known unknown.[8]

At first glance Bernard Lonergan might seem an unlikely candidate for inclusion in the train of authors reflecting on the transcendence of God. The 'calculating' tone of his proof for the existence of God in chapter 19 of *Insight* and the extended detail of his analogy for the divine based on the content of an unrestricted act of understanding in that chapter, linger on in our memory. Yet even within *Insight* Lonergan mentions approvingly Aquinas' position that all we have is knowledge that God is and knowledge of what God is not.[9] It remains a fact, however, that chapter 19 of *Insight* is not Lonergan's most accessible acclamation of the transcendence of God.

Lonergan's treatment of the notion of mystery is more indicative of his respect for the divine transcendence. In chapter 17 of *Insight* Lonergan investigates the sense of the unknown. Not any 'unknown' is in question but, like the Pseudo Dionysius, Lonergan too speaks of a 'known unknown'. By his use of this paradoxical expression Lonergan indicates that unknown which, on the basis of what we *do* know, is intended by our questions for *further* knowledge. He is indicating a dimension of human experience that takes us beyond the domesticated and the familiar. Thus the sphere of reality to which mystery belongs is attended by an 'undefined surplus of significance and momentousness'.[10]

Now in this early account of the notion of mystery in *Insight* Lonergan gave several indications of the direction in which this notion would develop in his later writings. The first is that he was moving towards an intensified consideration of the concomitance of mystery and affectivity.[11] Mystery's function is not merely cognitive. Already in *Insight* he could write: 'The achievement, then, of full understanding and the attainment even of the totality of correct judgments would not free man from the necessity of dynamic images that partly are symbols partly are signs.'[12] Important too is the role which the encounter with mystery plays in human authenticity. The finality inherent in the orientation to mystery belongs to the human as human; it is an intrinsic characteristic of each human being.[13] Let us now see how these two hints are taken up in his later work *Method in Theology*.

A distinction made by the expert on Neo-platonism, Arthur Hilary Armstrong, may be of help. He wrote: 'In considering the *via negativa* it is important to distinguish between the apophatic method of intellectual approach to God, or negative theology, and the experience of supreme transcendence (which is also deepest immanence) which impels to and is undergone in the search for ... the Divine mystery beyond speech or thought.'[14] In *Method in Theology* Lonergan's treatment of mystery is firmly linked to the sphere of religious *experience*.[15]

Religious experience is, according to Lonergan, an experience of the love of God flooding our hearts. On the dynamic state of being in love, he writes; 'Because the dynamic state is conscious without being known, it is an experience of mystery. Because it is being in love, the mystery is not merely attractive but fascinating; to it one belongs; by it one is possessed. Because it is unmeasured love, the mystery evokes awe.'[16] Here the affective side of the fascination of mystery receives the attention that was only present in inchoate form in *Insight*.

The early proof for God's existence and the analogy for the divine essence are complemented in *Method in Theology* by an account of the question of God and of the human questing for God. It is here that the hint in *Insight* arising from the finality of the orientation to mystery, the link between the full human development and the orientation to divine mystery, clearly emerges: 'Man's transcendental subjectivity is mutilated or abolished, unless he is stretching forth towards the intelligible, the unconditioned, the good of value. The reach, not of his attainment, but of his intending is unrestricted.'[17] The next sentence shows that this intending is ultimately an intending of the divine: 'There lies within his horizon a region for the divine, a shrine for ultimate holiness.'[18] He speaks of a native orientation to the divine.

2. The Human Outreach to the Divine

In many of his writings Bernard Lonergan emphasises a structure which he identifies in the conscious operations of the human. On the basis of this structure Lonergan can speak of a transcendental method, of a normative pattern of operations which underlies the intentional outreach of the human to all that is true, to all that is good, ultimately, to God. Many of the writers of the first Christian centuries also reflected on the human outreach to the divine.

Over one thousand six hundred years ago, the theologians known to us as the Cappadocian fathers reflected not only on the great mysteries of our faith, taking part in the trinitarian and pneumatological controversies of the fourth century, but also on the human journey to God, on spirituality.

Gregory of Nyssa in his Commentary on the Song of Songs offers us a reflection on the Christian interior life. Like Lonergan, Gregory drew attention to the dynamic outreach of the human to the infinite God and exhorted his readers 'not to stop in your tracks at the grasped but ever to seek more and not to stay put at that which has already been grasped.'[19] Again, commenting on 1 Corinthians 8:2, he points out that in the case of knowledge of God it is always so that the not yet understood is infinitely more than that which has been understood.[20] Using the famous image of a spring ever issuing forth out of the ground with fresh water and ever surprising its beholder with an unending supply of water, Gregory writes that the human wonders at the continuing revealing of God and is consumed by the desire to know more than that which has already been grasped.[21]

Thus Gregory of Nyssa is one of the tradition's best exponents of the human questing in the light of the divine mystery. The comparison of Lonergan and Gregory of Nyssa suggested itself because, among the early writers reflecting on God's transcendence, he in particular thematised the dynamic outreach of the human to the infinite God.

3. Knowledge Mediated through Discipleship
Another scriptural verse to which Gregory devoted attention is Exodus 33:23. Here God speaks to Moses and concedes that Moses can see the back of God. Gregory's comments on this verse do not represent a critical exegesis, but rather an interpretation, an interpretation steeped in experience of the spiritual journey. What, he asks, is this mysterious seeing God's back? His answer is one of the finest descriptions of the

interplay of discipleship and contemplation which the Christian tradition has bequeathed us:

> The one who desires to see God,
> sees the desired one through ever following
> and the contemplation of His face
> is the never ending going-towards-Him
> realised through closely following the Word.[22]

The expression 'the back of God' is understood as an indication that the longing for God is never ending. It is an affirmation of the infinity of our quest for God and the infinity of the divine essence. Those contours of the divine which we are privileged to recognise are given to us in the Word, and moreover in the Word as approached through discipleship. Desire, the thirst for more, is also highlighted as is the process of following, the ever-going-towards-Him. Gregory resolves the riddle of seeing God's back in terms of the circumincession of following and contemplation. The never ending quest for the knowledge of God is presented by Gregory in terms of the religious experience inherent in discipleship.

The nexus of discipleship and contemplation which is suggested by at least some of Gregory's texts bears comparison with Lonergan's position. In Lonergan's later writings intending the divine involves a holistic actualisation of the human subject engaging the cognitive, moral and religious levels of human intentionality. The later Lonergan was interested in the conscious appropriation of the subject of itself operating on each of the four levels of consciousness intentionality. He also came to speak of the phenomenon of conversion. By this term he indicates a vertical exercise of freedom involving a movement into a new horizon significant enough to involve a radical new beginning.[23]

In particular Lonergan speaks of three major conversions, intellectual, moral and religious. Intellectual conversion involves a rejection of the myth that knowing is like looking. Instead one attains a critical judgement of self-affirmation 'I am a knower,' wherein the three operations of cognitive activity, reaching a climax in the judgement, are affirmed. In moral conversion the shift is from a state of drifting to the dawning realisation that one is responsible for one's own actions. One realises that one is responsible not only for the actions, but, consequently for who one is. Religious conversion, Lonergan writes, is 'being grasped by ultimate concern. It is other-worldly falling in love. It is total and permanent self-surrender without conditions, qualifications, reservations.'[24]

Now there is a dynamic interaction of the conversions.[25] Lonergan speaks of the interrelations of the conversions in terms of the 'sublation' of one conversion by another. The sublating conversion goes beyond the sublated conversion, introduces something new and distinct, yet it does not interfere negatively with the sublated. On the contrary, not only does it need it, but it includes it and carries forward all the proper features of the other conversion to a fuller realisation.[26] One interaction to which Lonergan devotes particular attention is that of religious conversion and moral conversion. When a subject's heart has been flooded by the love of God that person experiences an intensified discernment of value and their decision-making is carried forward to a new realisation and the richer context of a love relationship with God. The moral life becomes the life of following, of discipleship. This richer context also becomes the context within which the subject seeks truth in general and the truth about God in particular. Both the religious conversion and the moral conversion 'sublate' the intellectual conversion of the subject. Expressing Lonergan's thought concretely we may say that in the thus converted subject, questing becomes a longing for the loving God, and just who that God is, 'God's identity' as it were, is hinted at by the very demands the divine love makes on those following as disciples.

Once again we can observe how the writings of Bernard Lonergan and Gregory of Nyssa support each other and mutually amplify the insight into the knowledge mediated by discipleship which each has expressed in his own categories. Gregory wrote about closely following the Word. Let us now turn to what Lonergan wrote about discipleship and Jesus Christ.

His essay 'The Mediation of Christ in Prayer' is outstanding in its emphasis on the mutual influencing of Christ and the Christian in the life of faith.[27] Now by 'prayer' Lonergan was not merely indicating the moments which one spends in *explicit* or *exclusive* devotion to the divine – in daily prayer or a liturgy or in a meditative reflection. Rather he invokes the 'Pray constantly' of 1 Thessalonians 5:17 and explains how the orientation to God extends to all our activities:

> In loving our neighbour we are loving Christ. In making ourselves good Christians and better Christians we are loving Christ. In this process, which is universal, which can regard every act, thought, word, or deed, and omission, there is a complete universality, a possibility of the complete growth of every aspect of the person.[28]

> The life of prayer is individual in its form. All the polymorphic and individual acts of living may be embraced within a prayerful orientation to Christ. An

individual collage of acts centring on Christ may thus emerge. The fruits which the life of prayer bears are also of an individual nature: prayer fosters authenticity. The acts of living and the acts within prayer are referred to Christ. By that process we perfect ourselves, we become ourselves, we become autonomous individuals...'[29]

In living towards Christ, in this mediation of Christ in the prayer-filled life we put on Christ as model and intended object of our love. An apprehension of Christ emerges which is intensely personal:

'It is Christ, not as apprehended by the apostles, by Paul and John, by the church, by Christ himself, by the Spirit; it is our *own* apprehension of him. It is, as it were, putting on, acquiring, our own view of him. We put on Christ in our own way, in accord with our own capacities and individuality, in response to our own needs and failings.'[30]

Gregory had used the model of following the Word. Lonergan uses that of putting on Christ. Both metaphors help to express the growth in knowledge which discipleship fosters.

In the foregoing I have linked Lonergan's thought with that of thinkers who belong to the patristic tradition. What may be gained from such a procedure? Familiarity with Lonergan's analysis of the structures inherent in the operations of the conscious subject alerts one to aspects of the anthropology of the fathers which have sometimes been overlooked. Reading the fathers of Christian spirituality, be they the fathers of the church in the classic meaning of this expression, or simply those women and men who have lived and taught the life of faith, draws attention to perennial aspects of Christian spirituality. Their heritage of musings, teaching, poetry is in turn a lens with which to rediscover key notions in Lonergan's writings. So a mutual amplification of some quieter tones results. The mutually supportive function of different voices of the Christian tradition communally engaged in a discernment of what it is to follow Christ thus emerges.

4. Lonergan and Contemporary Spirituality

On what level do the writings of Bernard Lonergan make a contribution to the analysis of contemporary spirituality?

Lonergan's transcendental method, involving as it does the appropriation of the conscious operations of the subject, is a fitting contemporary correlative of the classic imperative: 'know yourself'. With Lonergan we learned 'to do it', to experience, to understand, to judge, to fall in love, and to pay attention to these conscious acts on every level that this is possible. Here too we may regard Lonergan as heir to a tradition which valued introspection. Let me turn to the phrase *Attende tibi ipsi* in the Latin title of the homily of another fourth century Cappadocian theologian, St Basil of Caesarea (the brother of Gregory of Nyssa).[31] This title reminds us of the Greek maxim, know yourself, and we might be lulled into expecting a call to *reflect* on what it is to be a human. The homily does indeed expound on the dignity of the human, the human who is created in the image of God. Yet this homily witnesses to more. In the Greek title of the homily stand the words 'προσεχε σεαυτω': that tells us that the Latin *attende* stands here not in the sense of *know* but rather in the sense of watch out: catch a hold of yourself. In the biblical text being quoted (Deut. 15. 9) the exhortation is not to cheat, so we can interpret this 'Προσεχε' as a call to live according to the moral exigence of one's person. Here too we have another example of a patristic author advocating the integration of a purely cognitive perspective within a horizon of moral responsibility. The homily's long description of the wonder that the human person is, lives from the notion of a moral exigency to reach one's full potential not only as the creature invited to wonder but also as the creature summoned to love and act justly.

Important for the assessment of Lonergan's contemporary relevance is the imperative style which characterises the homily and Lonergan's writings alike: one is *called upon* to appropriate the dynamism intrinsic in one's knowing and loving. This injunctive moment in both authors cuts through contemporary accusations of relativism which might otherwise be raised against a given anthropological *theory*, a *theory* of what it is to be a human. Lonergan's transcendental method is a valuable tool for the study of spirituality in the atmosphere of relativism within which academic reflection now takes place.

How can Lonergan's ideas help contemporary believers in their everyday faith? We live in an age which casts great doubt on the power of any discourse to reach truth. Accordingly, any conception of God seems to be relative. Christians seem to have to choose between an extremely negative form of religion and of theology, on the one hand, and on the other hand, a God who is everything and anything. Both options present a God who is difficult to worship. Can one live without God, without an adequate concept of God? Or can one live with God, but with a shimmering, constantly changing concept of God? But must we speak of a corresponding receding *understanding* of God? Lonergan wrote extensively on the importance of overcoming a mere conceptualism and placing the act of understanding at the centre of our thinking in general and our theology in particular. He also highlighted what he called a self-correcting process of learning and spoke of the possibility of a critique of beliefs.[32] On the basis of his writings it is thus possible to affirm a continual process of self-correcting insight into who God is not. There are periods in the biographies of individuals which can benefit from an insight into the self-correcting process of learning. For example one might think here of the way first term students begin to study theology and sometimes reel when some of the cherished notions they thought central to their faith are then shown to be mere 'props' to an essential aspect of the faith. This process can be painful and it is good to be able to thematise what is going on. Teachers who have seen it again and again know the lean faith which emerges is unshakeable. Realising and thematising the process of learning to recognise an error as such can help students to attain to that mature faith.[33]

I have argued that Lonergan's transcendental method is a very valuable tool for those involved in reflecting on contemporary spirituality. But on the concrete level of living the faith too, he offers us help. The appropriation of the self-correcting process, as part of the dynamism at the core of the human person, can have a reassuring effect on 'doubting postmoderns'. When one makes this self-correcting process one's own, then it is the *progress in truth* which occupies the centre of attention. One is not scrupulously preoccupied with the old rejected 'error', with the notion which has been further refined or indeed corrected. Rather, the step forward to the more adequate insight is at the centre of attention.

Let me conclude with a picture for this progress taken from an adventure sport which has become popular:

quarrying. In this sport people select a sheer rock face and decked out with ropes and other equipment they set out to scale the wall. In this process their progress is given to them through their fingers which probe the rock face for a suitable higher ledge onto which they can hold on and lever themselves up. Their progress is given to them in the experience of their legs kicking off from a narrow ledge below, unfurling to bring them a metre higher. Progress is given in the experience of a rock face being scaled by their effort. There are moments of gratitude when their hand discovers a ledge they can really grip onto, when the mountain seems to be kind to them. A person scaling such a cliff feels their progress in their limbs and fingers, not by looking back over their shoulder at what they have left behind.

In the precipitous searching of a doubting age, Christians are given an experience of progress through a creative refining of their understanding of God. It is important to appropriate this progress as such, and not to become too preoccupied with what has been left behind. The lower rock-face now has value as a way already taken.

Notes

1   An earlier version of this paper is due to appear under the title 'Following the Back of God: A Reflection on Lonergan's Notion of Mystery', in Fred Lawrence, ed., *Lonergan Workshop*, Atlanta, Georgia: Scholars Press, forthcoming. The original paper has been significantly modified and expanded.

2   See Graham Greene, The Lost Childhood, in: *Collected Essays*, London: Vintage, 1999, pp. 13-18, here p. 17.

3   For a good introduction to negative theology, see Deirdre Carabine, *The Unknown God. Negative Theology in the Platonic Tradition: Plato to Eriugena*, Louvain Theological and Pastoral Monographs, 19, Louvain: Peeters Press/Eerdmans, 1995.

4   Behind the pseudonym lies most probably a Syrian author of the late fifth and early sixth century. See Andrew Louth, *Denys the Areopagite*, Outstanding Christian Thinkers Series, London: Geoffrey Chapman, 1989.

5   'I have praised the main notions of affirmative theology', Ps. Dionysius, De mystica theologia, III, in: *Corpus Dionysiacum II*, Günter Heil, A. M. Ritter eds., Patristische Texte und Studien, 36, Berlin: de Gruyter, 1991, p. 146, 1-2. Here my translation: compare the translation of Colm Luibheid in: *Pseudo-Dionysius. The Collected Works*, New York, Mahwah: Paulist Press, 1987, p. 138.

6   See Carabine, *The Unknown God*, p. 2 and compare Paul Rorem, *Pseudo-Dionysius. A Commentary on the Texts and an Introduction to Their Influence*, Oxford: Oxford University Press, 1993.

7   Epistula 3, in: *Corpus Dionysiacum II*, Günter Heil, A. M. Ritter ed., p. 159, 7.

8   Epistula 3, in: *Corpus Dionysiacum II*, Günter Heil, A. M. Ritter ed., p. 159, 9-10.

9   *CWL*, 3, p. 757.

10   *Insight*, p. 556.

11   ..'. [I]t will be well to distinguish between the image as image, the image as symbol, and the image as sign. The image as image is the sensible content as operative on the sensitive level; it is the image inasmuch as it functions within the psychic syndrome of associations, affects, exclamations, and articulated speech and actions. The image as symbol or as sign is the image as standing in correspondence with activities or elements on the intellectual

level. But as symbol, the image is linked simply with the paradoxical 'known unknown.' As sign, the image is linked with some interpretation that offers to indicate the import of the image.' *Insight*, p. 557.

12   *Insight*, pp. 570/571.

13   On p. 557 of *Insight* Lonergan speaks of a 'directed but, in a sense, indeterminate dynamism.'

14   A. H. Armstrong, 'Apophatic-Kataphatic Tensions in Religious Thought from the Third to the Sixth Century AD: A Background to Augustine and Eriugena', in: F. X. Martin and J. A. Richmond, eds., *From Augustine to Eriugena. Essays on Neoplatonism and Christianity in Honour of John O' Meara*, Washington, 1991, pp. 12-21, here, p. 12.

15   This paper cannot treat Lonergan's writings on the 'mysteries' in the plural. See *Method*, p. 349.

16   *Method*, p. 106.

17   *Method*, p. 103.

18   *Method*, p. 103.

19   *Gregorii Nysseni, In Canticum canticorum homiliae*, H. Langerbeck, ed., Leiden: Brill, 1960, p. 352.

20   *Ibid.*, p. 321.

21   *Ibid.*

22   *Ibid.*, p. 356.

23   See *Method*, pp. 237-38ff.

24   *Method*, p. 240. For a critical discussion of Lonergan's notion of religious conversion see my *The Liberation of Consciousness. Bernard Lonergan's Theological Foundations in Dialogue with the Theological Aesthetics of Hans Urs von Balthasar*, Frankfurt: Verlag Josef Knecht, 1992, pp. 110-14.

25   Compare Bernard Lonergan, 'Self-transcendence: Intellectual, Moral, Religious', in: *CWL*, 17, pp. 313-31, esp. pp. 330-31.

26   *Method*, p. 241.

27   'The Mediation Christ in Prayer', *CWL*, 6, pp. 160-82.

28   'The Mediation of Christ in Prayer', p. 180.

29   *Ibid.*, p. 182.

30   *Ibid.*, p. 180.

31   'In illud: 'Attende tibi ipsi'.' The critical edition of the Greek text is *L'Homélie de Basile de Césarée sur le mot 'observe-toi toi-meme.' Édition critique du texte grec et étude sur la tradition manuscrite*, S. Y. Rudberg ed.,

Stockholm: Almqvist & Wiksell, 1962, (Acta Universitatis Stockholmiensis. Studia Graeca Stockholmiensia, 2).

32   See for example the section, 'The Critique of Beliefs' in chapter XX of *Insight* .

33   The combination of this insight into a progression in the appropriation of truth and an unrelenting affirmation of the mystery surrounding God provides the *decisive link* between the theology of Bernard Lonergan and the *theologia negativa* of the past. Neither Lonergan nor a Pseudo Dionysius wish to deny the possibility of truth. The problem is not 'no truth' but 'too much truth.' The fitting reaction is not denial, but progressive appropriation. Here Gregory of Nyssa's insight into the infinite outreach to the infinite God is complementary. For Lonergan mystery is a *known* unknown. This knowledge can take on many different forms; it can be more experiential, it can be given to us in the words of scripture, or elucidated in theoretic form in systematic theology, yet common to all these forms of knowing is the openness for further questions.

CHAPTER TEN

Spirituality and Religious Experience: A Perspective from Rahner

—— Philip Endean ——

Introduction

Karl Rahner had a habit of transforming the subjects which he discussed. His fans often present him as a figure who adapted Catholic tradition to the modern world. But friends like these only make his critics' case appear more plausible. I believe we should read him rather differently, rather more creatively. He worked within the rather strange world of Austrian and German universities, regulated by concordat between the state and the Holy See. As a professor in such locations, he was in the modern academy without being quite of it. And he used that position to challenge and subvert the Enlightenment canons of truth and rationality prevalent not only in the academy of his day, but also – for all its fulminations against 'modernism' – in the official Church. He anticipated, I believe, the elements of salutary truth in today's theological critiques of modernity, while admirably avoiding the elements of irrationality and pretentiousness often to be found in such critiques. Elsewhere in this collection, Dermot Lane hints at convergences between the programmes of Rahner and Derrida, and Declan Marmion has made some more general suggestions about how Rahner appears in a postmodern intellectual world. I would go further, and describe Rahner as a postmodern thinker *avant la lettre* – at least to the extent that postmodern theology retains contact with sanity and clarity.

1. Subverting Subdisciplines

One sign of how Rahner's vision was intellectually subversive is his ranging across the various disciplines studied in a theological faculty, sometimes to the irritation of his colleagues. He produced insights that undermined the legitimations of academic fiefdoms, and called into question the assumptions determining the very identity of theological disciplines.

A clear example of what I mean can be found in Rahner's celebrated concept of the supernatural existential. We naturally, even now, think of it as primarily a contribution to the dogmatic theology of grace. It had its origins in Rahner's activity as professor for the old treatise, *De gratia*. But even in the 1950 essay where the concept receives its classic articulation,[1] it is already clear that this insight undermines the standard conception of philosophy as a discipline conducted without any reference to Christian revelation. I have no way of knowing what 'in my existential experience of myself' falls 'within the realm of my "nature" and would also exist, exist in just this form, if there were no vocation to supernatural communion with God.' If we try to do a transcendental deduction purely philosophically,

> ... even then one does not know whether one may not have introduced too little into this concept of humanity, or whether in the very act of answering the question, contingently but for us unavoidably, a supernatural element may not have been at work ...

which could never in actual fact be bracketed off, and so would prevent one from laying hold *purely* of humanity's natural essence.[2]

As Anne Carr puts the matter, pure philosophy for Rahner is as much a remainder concept as pure nature.[3] It can never be securely isolated. Later, in the *Grundkurs*, Rahner would make basically the same point by insisting that his method involves a blurring of the distinction between fundamental and dogmatic theology.[4] Rahner is subverting a distinction between reason and revelation that nevertheless underlay the conventional discourse both of Church theology and of the modern academy. For a serious Christian theologian, pure philosophy as standardly conceived was incoherent.

It is, of course, true that Rahner was a theologian concerned with what traditionally falls under the heading of spirituality. It is also true that experience – religious experience if we must – plays a foundational role in his thought. The text that he called his spiritual testament,[5] 'Ignatius Loyola speaks to a Modern Jesuit', centres on the theme of the immediate experience of God:

> I experienced God, the nameless and unsearchable one, silent yet near, in the Trinity which is His turning to me. ... Godself. Godself I experienced: not human words about God. God, and the sovereign freedom that is proper to God, the freedom that can only be experienced as coming from God, not from the intersection of earthly realities and calculations. [. . .] That's what it was, I say. Indeed, I would say this: you can have the same experience too ... the truth remains: God is able and willing to deal immediately with His creature; the fact that this occurs is something that

human beings can experience happening; they can
apprehend the sovereign disposing of God's freedom
over their lives and appropriate it – a disposing that
objective argument 'from below' cannot predict as a law
of human reason, neither philosophically, nor
theologically nor arguing from experience.[6]

The temptation is for us to read such a passage simply as a
call for theology to pay more attention to spirituality, to the
experiential aspect of Christian life, and to see Rahner as
merely as a model for this. I want to suggest that such
accounts of the matter are far too complacent and
conservative, and sell Rahner's genius short. Just as the
concept of the supernatural existential exposes the limitations
of a purely dogmatic theology somehow in a separate
compartment from fundamental theology and philosophy of
religion, so Rahner's insistence that God's own self can be
experienced is pointing us to how the reality expressed by
theology transcends disjunctions between speculative and
practical reason.

Spirituality is not something secondary, a mere response
to a truth established by some other means, or a mere
application of what can be known already; and nor is
Rahner's use of spirituality language merely a plea that such
a response be taken more seriously. Rahner's point is richer.
Our ongoing experience of grace, conventionally thought
of back then in terms of ascetical and mystical theology and
more recently in terms of spirituality, just is an element in
the reality of grace, conventionally articulated as an aspect
of dogmatic theology. A consistent theology incorporates
both the theoretical and the practical; they cannot be
cleanly separated. To echo Kant: Christian ideas without
Christian practice and spirituality are empty; Christian

practice and spirituality without Christian ideas are blind. Theology needs to be reconceived as involving both; it is not purely or primarily a speculative activity. The study of what we now call spirituality was important for Rahner because what he learnt in that context led him to reconstruct what counted as theology. A Rahnerian perspective on spirituality and religious experience will certainly stress the importance of these realities – but at the same time it will be challenging assumptions often built in to the ways in which these slippery concepts are being used.

Put in those terms, the point sounds abstract – not really suited to the pragmatic temper of theology in these islands. The main reason for the abstractness is that this aspect of Rahner's message about the nature of theology has not really been taken on board – the biggest single reason why there are so many misreadings of his message in the secondary literature. But let me try to explain the point more directly by answering my brief directly, and offering a Rahnerian perspective on spirituality and religious experience.

2. Beyond Kerygmatic Theology

It has often been noted that Rahner's first published work was a brief meditation, 'Why We Still Need to Pray',[7] and there are many pious stories in circulation about Rahner's commitment to the life of prayer. My favourite, perhaps because I was a witness, is of when he came to Heythrop College in London for his eightieth birthday party in Feburary 1984. The gathering centered on a guest lecture in his honour by the distinguished Oxford theologian, John Macquarrie, and many notable people were present. Rahner sat on the podium. He did not understand English well, and his physical health by this stage was such that he tired easily. At a certain point he stopped trying to listen to the lecture.

Instead, quite visibly, he shuffled; he took his rosary out of his pocket; and he began to tell the proverbial beads.

The Rahner literature and oral tradition contains many stories in this vein. But we need to be careful when we tell them, careful about what is going on when it is said that a theologian is a holy man, that a theology is somehow 'spiritual', or 'nourished by prayer', or 'on its knees', or 'in living contact with spirituality'. At its worst, such talk is manipulative: an attempt to pass off a shoddy argument or a conventional position as valid by exploiting people's trust and good will. More often, it undermines critical thinking: the pious imagination can seize on an image like that of Rahner praying the rosary on a public platform and reassure itself that theology is fundamentally harmless, that it will not change anything. Rahner thinks 'spirituality' important for rather different reasons. It is not that Rahner brought theology back into contact with 'spirituality'; rather, he saw the two as fundamentally identical. The study of theology just is the study of God's dealings with humanity, dealings which are continuing, dealings which we discover in our experience. And the importance of 'prayer' in theology is not a matter of any hare-brained belief that piety can substitute for serious thinking, nor of reassurance for the devout that theology is not after all so threatening. Prayer is important for theology because the living contact with God that it betokens is an absolutely vital source for theology, an indispensable *locus theologicus*; it should be providing the energy to move our whole being, including our intellect, beyond the conventional and familiar into something new.

Rahner's achievement centred on a belief that grace was something we could experience. Though lived Catholic spirituality even since the Renaissance and Reformation had often been rich and exuberant, the theology into which Karl

Rahner was educated in the 1920s and 1930s was reticent about spiritual experience. It had been decisively shaped by a Counter-Reformation reaction against Protestantism, in particular against the possibility that a person's private experience of God could serve as a source of religious authority overriding the Church's official leaders. Thus standard Catholic theology tended to understand the presence of God among us as something in principle beyond our experience: we could only *believe* that it was true, on the basis of a message taught us by someone else. In an interview given a couple of months before he died in 1984, Rahner spoke of how he saw his theology differing from that of previous tradition in general and of his own teachers in particular:

> I have, in my own theology ... over and over again drawn attention to how there is such a thing as the experience of grace. My teacher ... Hermann Lange ... was strongly opposed to this kind of thing. Lange did, relentlessly, defend the idea of a so-called 'sanctifying, real (*seinshafte*) grace'. However, in his view, this grace lay absolutely beyond consciousness. According to this tradition one could only know *about* it, through external revelation and sacred scripture.[8]

Rahner argued for his alternative position in two ways. Firstly, he appealed to scripture and tradition: we are taught, quite simply, that God is God-with-us, that God establishes peace among us, that the fruits of the Spirit can and do make a difference to how we experience our lives. Secondly, the idea of grace (or anything else) could exist without *ever*, in *any* way, being in principle able to modify human awareness is self-contradictory; if you can speak of grace at all, you cannot be denying that you are aware of it, either in yourself or another, affecting your consciousness. If grace exists at all, it exists as a reality of human experience. The experience may be very hard to name or recognise, and the reality of grace may not be accepted. But if God in Christ has become human, then, in the words of one of Rahner's early prayers, God has also become human experience. Rahner is insisting, therefore, not only that God dwells among human beings, but also that human awareness is capable of 'touching our Creator and Lord'. For Rahner, this principle became central.

For Rahner, therefore, 'the mystical' and 'spirituality' must be allowed to shape our understanding of theology, indeed of reality, *as a whole*. This was why he did not allow himself to become a conventional 'spiritual writer' or 'spiritual theologian'. Instead he used what he learnt from the great spiritual masters he studied as a young man – Ignatius Loyola, of course, but also writers from the early church such as Evagrius and Gregory of Nyssa, and medieval spiritual writers such as Ruusbroec, Tauler, Eckhart and Bonaventure – as inspiration for the study of theology as such. Spirituality was too important and too central to be a mere specialism.

We can see the youthful Rahner being guided by this conviction as he began to feel his way through the multiple and arcane sensitivities that mark the internal politics of any theology faculty. When he arrived in Innsbruck, he found his own elder brother, Hugo, at the centre of a movement for what was called 'kerygmatic theology': – a second kind of theology existing alongside 'academic' theology. Whereas 'academic' theology would focus on the truth of God's own self, 'kerygmatic' theology would work with different methods, and focus more on the God who can be preached. It seems clear that Karl Rahner at least flirted with the movement; he published in its journal.[9] But, relatively early, he parted company with it; it may be significant that his early articles on and within kerygmatic theology are only being republished now, after his death. 'Kerygmatic' should not be used to designate *one part* of theology; it refers to *an aspect of all* theology.

He reminisced on this decision twenty-five years later, in a brief dictionary article.[10] 'Kerygmatic' theology was founded on assumptions that seemed ridiculous (at least to a believer) once you named them. The distinction between the two sorts of theology seemed to imply that God's own self was somehow different from the God-for-us proclaimed by the Gospel. It also implied that you could know the truth about God without that truth somehow involving you, challenging you, transforming you:

> Rightly, this theory found no acceptance. *All* theology must be theology of salvation. It is impossible and illegitimate for there to be a theology which is merely 'theoretical', fundamentally uncommitted.

While criticizing the movement – and by this stage (1961) it was a historical curiosity – Rahner nevertheless went on to highlight three important concerns that it represented:

> But this is not to gainsay a threefold basic concern underlying this initiative, a concern which is not yet satisfied:
> - a good part of contemporary scholastic theology does not stand sufficiently clearly in the service of a really living proclamation, meeting the human person of today and his or her faith-need.
> - today's theological academic goings-on in the universities do too little to train the young pastoral clergy for their tasks.

- the kerygma itself cannot just be a merely simplified version of academic theology, even if this theology is correct as far as it goes.

It is worth making two observations about this small article. Firstly, though Rahner rejects 'kerygmatic theology' (modern equivalents would be 'pastoral theology' or 'practical theology'), he identifies nevertheless three legitimate concerns informing the project. Karl Rahner was not deaf to these concerns. An essay he wrote in the 1960s is entitled, 'The New Claims which Pastoral Theology Makes upon Theology as a Whole' – a title that says much about how Rahner understood his own intellectual vocation. Karl Rahner took the concerns behind 'kerygmatic theology' as a stimulus to renew theology *as a whole*. That it is *human beings* who know the truth of God is not something theologically incidental, somehow independent of the content of that truth. God is God-with-us; God's reality incorporates us; and therefore our learning, our growth into the life of God, is, under grace, constitutive of God's very identity. Moreover, when the word is preached effectively, when – for instance – someone truly hears the proclamation, 'your sins are forgiven you', something new happens within the life history of that person. Theology may indeed be able to name this reality, but it cannot determine in advance what it will be and how it will play itself out. For each person's history is unique and unrepeatable: the word of God is still alive and active.

Secondly, Rahner's grounds for denying the legitimacy of a 'kerygmatic' theology are not the standard ones. Plenty of theological academics, even now, are sniffy about the 'pastoral' aspects of theology. *Pastoralia* – to use a quaint word still current in the UK – is often patronized as a soft underbelly of theology, somewhat suspect in comparison to the hard, objective study of Bible and dogma, a back door into the academy allowing access to subjective and emotional realities that have no proper place there. But Rahner's objection is different: he is challenging the claim of *any* theology to mere 'objectivity'. If theology is about the incomprehensible God who is yet *our* God on whom we depend, it cannot simply operate with the methods and conventions of an Enlightenment science like Newtonian physics, that presupposes a 'neutral' observer and operates with objective facts. Rahner was not challenging the distinction between theology-in-itself and theology-for-people because he was worried about theology-for-people being somehow too subjective, too difficult to handle. He wanted, rather, to insist that – at least on a Christian account of the matter – theology-for-people is the only theology there is: the study of a God who is permanently and irrevocably God-with-us. In other words, what needed to be challenged were the assumptions behind 'academic' or 'scholarly' theology. Once those illusions are exposed, the only problem with 'practical theology' or 'kerygmatic theology' is that the adjectives add no real content to the noun.

The issues about 'kerygmatic theology' and 'pastoral theology' apply also to what in English is the newer and much more popular term 'spirituality'. It is not that Rahner was first a theologian and then a holy man as a kind of extra, by coincidence as it were. Rather, the reflective activity we call theology, and the emotional and relational process we call spiritual growth, are two aspects of one fundamental reality: the growth of the whole human person towards God. Because theology is a self-implicating discipline, a creative theology will have 'spiritual' meaning: people who read it and hear it aright will be challenged by it, changed by it. Good spiritual direction helps people make a decent theology out of their own experience – however much it is true that defensive resistance to the Spirit often takes the form of 'intellectualization' and that spiritual directors are not always being just flaky or irresponsible when they tell people to get out of their heads into their hearts. Conversely, even if a mainstream 'spiritual' figure, an Ignatius or a Thérèse, writes in a crude, theologically uneducated way, the very fact that they are prophetic and creative implies that they set an agenda for *theology*. What makes them different from the holy people to be found both within and outside any Christian community is that their experience and writings enable us somehow to break new ground in *understanding* and *knowing* God. There was indeed justification for making Thérèse a doctor of the church. The witness of the saints, whether canonised or not, is itself a theological reality. That, for Rahner, was why 'spirituality' was important – not as an alternative to reflective theology, but rather as the animating principle of reflective theology, and indeed both its source and its goal.

3. Beyond 'Religious Experience'

In addressing more specifically the issue of 'religious experience', I shall allow myself to go into narrative mode. I can still remember the experience of reading for the first time a passage at the beginning of *Hörer des Wortes*:

> ... for a Thomistic metaphysics, the knowledge of God, on which a philosophy of religion that aspires to be more than merely descriptive *Religionsgeschichte* and religious psychology essentially depends, and in which it has already reached its goal, is not a self-contained academic discipline, but an aspect intrinsic to general metaphysics as such, to general ontology.[11]

I was in Innsbruck, at the outset of a year when I would discover aspects of theology that English gentlemen did not talk about. Of course I had studied philosophy, and even in the United Kingdom I had been taught some metaphysics. But 'metaphysics' and so-called 'philosophy of religion' had been separate courses. 'Religion' – an eminently criticisable abstraction on other grounds – had been discussed philosophically in a way quite divorced from the more general account of why things were as they were.[12] The operative definition of religion had been close to that of William James:

> Religion shall mean for us the feelings, acts, and experiences of individual men in their solitude, so far as they apprehend themselves to stand in relation to whatever they may consider the divine.[13]

Rahner's monstrous sentence was challenging this. For Rahner, the mystery of God is the mystery of reality, of all reality (surely a better word in English than the hermetic 'Being'). By contrast, James's ostensibly liberal and open-minded vision depends on a restriction, a restriction to how people 'apprehend themselves' in relation to *whatever they may consider* the divine; when all is said and done, his demonstrations of 'religion' outside Christianity amount to the claim that even in the most distant cultures one can find secularised versions of Lutheranism.

There are obvious points to be made here about realism and objectivity. But there is also an important point about the spiritual life. A Jamesian vision – to which there are many parallels in more recent literature – crucially limits the study of spirituality to what people *think* is true about themselves and whatever they call God – 'so far as they apprehend'; it leaves at best only marginal room for claims that any serious Christian study of spirituality will want to make: namely, that we are in the process of being transformed; our perspectives are thus shifting and are not definitive of what counts as true; if the spiritual life is being led seriously, our understanding of who we are will be permanently susceptible to change. We cannot legitimately structure a study of *God's* truth in such a way that our present constructions of that truth are axioms.

Moreover, even any coherent 'consideration' of the divine is likely to be universal. Rahner is famous precisely for having insisted that the grace of Christ is not confined within ecclesial conventionalities. This claim is rooted in a conviction about God's presence in human experience as a whole; clearly, experience is in one sense foundational to Rahner's thought. But everything depends on the fact that Rahner avoided a Jamesian idea of *religious* experience as one sort of experience among others. Rahner's invocation of experience was theologically productive precisely in its insistence that the reality of grace is always greater than *any* construction of it. Only if that is the case can the study of spirituality be a study of what gives growth, what transforms.

Once again, therefore, the same pattern: experience is important, but not just religious experience. God speaks through all experience. If a particular experience has special significance, it need not necessarily take a conventionally religious form. Moreover, and more importantly, it will always be pointing us forward and outward, and always disclosing to us what was – to use a standard Rahnerian phrase – 'always already' the case.

4. Rahner, Spirituality and the Contemporary Academy

Let me finish by offering some reflections on what these ideas of Rahner look like amid contemporary developments in the university world, both in Ireland and further afield. For a number of reasons, it is difficult for anyone to do theology well these days in a university setting. Governments are increasingly insisting on a utilitarian, economics-driven model of education, policed by questionnaires about measurable outcomes that undermine a Humanities education, let alone a theological one. We are faced with increasing demands to spend our energy on ticking meaningless boxes in forms rather than on thinking and teaching. Then there is the older problem of a secular academy and with the commitment to a definite tradition of revelation essential, by definition, to Christian theology. And Church authorities have bad days from time to time when they see the function of theology as merely to prate the conventionalities of the catechism, rather than creatively to explore the tradition and innovatively to evangelize an ever changing human reality.

Elsewhere in this collection, Eamonn Conway gives us a brilliant exposition of how the configuration of these difficulties is changing in contemporary Ireland, but he does not deny the existence of any of these problems, Given these struggles, given the toll they take, there are certainly pragmatic rationales for continuing, despite all I have said, to regard 'spirituality' as somehow different from theology as such. Some of these are perhaps not very high-minded. Firstly, spirituality tends to attract bums onto benches, and hence makes money when theology does not; I myself will confess to marketing the journal of theological education that I edit as a journal of spirituality, simply because there has been so much bad theology in good people's experience that the very word 'theology' can be off-putting. Secondly, in a world where there are anxieties about Church authority, talk of spirituality may provide a more or less justifiable way of sidestepping some of the obstacles, and disguising the subversiveness proper to responsible theology. Thirdly, an 'institute of spirituality' may provide a place for aspects of the theological enterprise that many a university department, overinfluenced by rationalism, refuses to take seriously. From all that I have said, it follows that the proper place for the study of spirituality – in all its methodological and interdisciplinary richness – lies within dogmatic theology. But it is hard to find anyone with any administrative responsibility for theology who would even understand that claim, let alone accept it – and there are then further serious issues about timetabling and resources. The obvious pragmatic solution, however intellectually problematic, is for something called 'spirituality' to be emancipated from 'theology' and to be pursued in a conventicle somewhere else, perhaps in a hospitable department of pastoral studies. After all, the important thing is that the spiritual life be studied seriously somewhere; it is only a secondary question how and where that study occurs.

Whatever we make of those pragmatic issues, I want to suggest that Rahner's work was shaped by an option *not* to cultivate spirituality as an enterprise separate from the life of faith, but rather to take the witness of the Church's holy people as a stimulus for the permanent transformation of theology as such. Rahner's high reputation has arisen largely from particular consequences of that option in ecclesiology, the theology of grace, Christology, the doctrine of God, and so on. But the fundamental option he took has been neither understood nor accepted by subsequent theologians, not even by the 'progressives' who idolize him.

Rahner's centenary year falls within the wintry time for the Church that he prophesied so tellingly, and also in a time of profound changes in educational systems that he did not foresee, changes radically inimical to theology as he imagined it, and indeed to humane education generally. Eamonn Conway's essay insists that the Gospel gives us no alternative but to plunge ourselves into the Babylon that is the contemporary university scene – we have to proclaim the Word amid our reality as it is; if we do not like that reality, we can only rely on the Gospel promise. I find here a salutary challenge to my own perfectionism, and its tendency when frustrated to lead me into a mild depression – a challenge for which I am grateful, and which I shall try to remember.

But at the same time, we cannot just go native in this Babylon. A responsible theology like Rahner's will always be challenging our culture in the name of the Gospel. For all the differences between his world and ours, we can learn much from what he was able to formulate in the seminary culture of pre-Conciliar European Roman Catholic theology – a culture which had strengths that ours lacks, even if we must also bear in mind its appalling repressiveness and what was at best its ambiguous response to Nazism and Fascism. What Rahner gave us – and let me here mention also Lonergan, Congar and our other theological centenarian, John Courtney Murray – should serve as a spur to divine dissatisfaction, and as a stimulus to our dreaming: a source of creative nostalgia as we keep trying to sing the Lord's song on alien soil.

Notes

1   See Nikolaus Schwerdtfeger, *Gnade und Welt: Zum Grundgefüge von Karl Rahners Theorie der 'anonymen Christen'*, Freiburg: Herder, 1982, pp. 164-69.

2   'Concerning the Relationship between Nature and Grace', *TI* 1, pp. 297-17.

3   Anne Carr, 'Theology and Experience in the Thought of Karl Rahner', *Journal of Religion*, 53 (1975), pp. 359-76, here p. 364.

4   *FCF*, p. 9 – compare the statements on the first pages of the text proper, pp. 24-25: 'a specific kind of interlocking between philosophy and theology'; 'A philosophy that is absolutely free of theology is not even possible in our historical situation.'

5   See an interview comment in Georg Sporschill, ed., *Bekenntnisse: Rückblick auf 80 Jahre*, Vienna: Herold, 1984, p. 58

6   Translations from my edition of Karl Rahner, *Spiritual Writings*, Maryknoll: Orbis, 2004, pp. 37, 38, 40.

7   For an English translation, see Karl Rahner, *Spiritual Writings*, pp. 31-33.

8   John Macquarrie, 'The Anthropological Approach to Theology', *Heythrop Journal*, 25 (1984), pp. 272-87. This text includes a record of questions put by Rahner to Macquarrie on the basis of his lecture, and Macquarrie's replies.

9   *Glaube in winterlicher Zeit: Gespräche mit Karl Rahner aus den letzten Lebensjahren*, eds., Paul Imhof and Hubert Biallowons, Düsseldorf: Patmos, 1986, p. 29. The interview from which this quotation is taken was not included in the English version of this volume.

10   For a much fuller and more technical development of these arguments, see Rahner's 1939 essay, 'Some Implications of the Scholastic Concept of Uncreated Grace', *TI* 1, pp. 321-46.

11   Rahner adapts this phrase from Ignatius Loyola in the first piece he ever published, reproduced below as the Prologue to the anthology. The Ignatian echoes in this piece are thoroughly and convincingly discussed in Arno Zahlauer, *Karl Rahner und sein 'produktives Vorbild' Ignatius von Loyola*, Innsbruck: Tyrolia, 1996, pp. 86-93. For the general issue of Rahner's links with Ignatius, see also my *Karl Rahner and Ignatian Spirituality*, Oxford: Oxford University Press, 2001; Zahlauer's discussion is summarized at pp. 28-29.

12   'Die deutsche protestantische Christologie der Gegenwart,' *Theologie der Zeit*, 1 (1936), pp. 189-202. The text has been reproduced in *SaW* 4, pp. 299-312.

13   *Lexikon für Theologie und Kirche*, second edition, vol. 6, p. 126. Now reprinted in *SaW*, 17/1, p. 313, typography PE. See also a fuller article which Rahner published in a Hungarian journal in 1941: 'Über die Verkündigungstheologie', in *SaW*, 4, pp. 337-45. On the movement more generally, see Hugo Rahner, *A Theology of Proclamation*, translated and adapted by various Jesuit hands, New York: Herder, 1967 (1st pub 1939).

14   *HW* 1, p. 15, *SaW*, 4, p. 14. Donceel's translation on p.4 rather mangles the text.

15   Subsequently, I have learnt much on the necessary distinctions here from Nicholas Lash, notably from his *Easter in Ordinary: Reflections on Human Experience and the Knowledge of God*, London: SCM, 1988, and the collection of essays, *The Beginning and End of 'Religion'*, Cambridge: Cambridge University Press, 1996.

16   *The Varieties of Religious Experience*, in various editions, near the beginning of lecture 2.

CHAPTER ELEVEN

Rahner and Lonergan on Spirituality[*]

—— Raymond Moloney ——

Introduction

When the famous names, Karl Rahner and Bernard Lonergan, are placed side by side, what first comes to mind is all that they held in common. They were strict contemporaries in the theological scene, both born in 1904 and both dying in the same year at the age of eighty. They were both Jesuits, educated at a time when the system of formation was remarkably uniform throughout their order. Both have been described as transcendental theologians, being influenced to an extent by Joseph Maréchal and by his reaction to Kantian philosophy. Despite however these points in common the two men are divided by very different systems of thought, and it is more the contrast than the comparison between them which this chapter wishes to explore.

The area within which this contrast will be examined is that of spirituality. The writings of Rahner in this area are well known, and several of them will be referred to in the course of this article. Lonergan, on the other hand, has rarely addressed the problems of spirituality directly, though there

* This article originally appeared in *Louvain Studies* 28 (2003), pp. 295-310.

is an increasing interest in the implications of his general position in theology and philosophy for this particular field.[1]

1. Transcendental and Categorial

The philosophy and theology of Karl Rahner are dominated by the distinction between the transcendental and the categorial, which applies across the whole field of theological reflection. By the transcendental we refer to the orientation to being, which is the mainspring of that pre-apprehension of all reality, from which all our particular acts of knowledge proceed. The categorial, a term inspired by Aristotle's categories, refers to the sphere of the concrete, namely to the world of particular beings and objects on which our transcendental orientation to being finally comes to rest and which it illumines as objects of our knowledge. According to the principle of this analysis, transcendental and categorial are essentially interdependent and may never be separated in practice, no more than the colours which light illumines can be separated from the light itself.

While Rahner always acknowledges that principle whenever he exposes the theory,[2] many commentators have felt that he often fails to do justice to the principle in practice. At times he seems to isolate, and, to an extent, to over-value the transcendental aspect of things to the neglect of the categorial.[3] In a recent book, Philip Endean remarks that in his later years Rahner would often speak of the permanent tension in his theology arising from its two starting-points, the transcendental and the categorial. In a private conversation he confessed that he did not know how they fitted together,[4] and in another place he speaks of dependence on the categorial as an imprisonment.[5]

In fact more commentators than Endean have been uneasy with this aspect of Rahner's work. The point around which most of these concerns have gathered is probably the famous hypothesis of the anonymous Christian.[6] Does this approach so emphasize the individual's invisible access to salvation that there is little or no need for the categorial, namely for the Church and its mission? Is there so much experience of God in the ordinary life of grace that any urgency about recourse to the sacraments is nullified? Striking a balance between the transcendental and the categorial is one of the basic issues in any assessment of Rahner's theology. Is it simply a question of tension, or does it sometimes reach the point of inconsistency? Balthasar once remarked that there are many Karl Rahners![7]

2. Two Issues for Contrast

However the subject of this article concerns Lonergan as well as Rahner, and at this stage we must see how he fits into the picture. There are two issues in particular which will enable us to bring out the contrast between the two authors. The first arises within ethics and moral theology. It concerns the relationship between the general principles of moral behaviour and how these are applicable to particular situations. The second issue comes from the *Spiritual Exercises* of St Ignatius and the procedure described there for discerning God's will in the particular decisions of life. Rahner himself suggests a parallel between these two issues, and indeed maintains that Ignatius has given us an important clue in breaking the mould of traditional essentialist and deductivist ethics.

a) *The Logic of Decision-Making*

The discussion of the ethical issue takes as its starting-point the rise of Situation Ethics, against which Rahner wished to develop his own proposal.[8] The problem concerned how the general principles of morality and natural law could be applied to any particular case. Rahner was reacting against what he called a syllogistic or essentialist ethics in the Catholic tradition, which he regarded as over-confident that concrete moral decisions could be arrived at by a process of deduction from the general principles of morality. This, he felt, often does not do justice to the complexities of the concrete situation and the way God's call to the individual has to take account of what is unique in the situation. 'God is interested in history, not only in so far as it is the putting into practice of norms, but also in so far as it is an unrepeatable unity and precisely thus of significance for salvation.'[9] Rahner appealed to Ignatius' principles of discernment as a paradigm for his own proposal, and in this way he felt that he was able to see some truth in Situation Ethics without falling under the strictures this system had received in the teaching of the Pope of the day, Pius XII.

In all this Rahner had in mind how all discursive reasoning rests ultimately on a grasp of first principles. These principles are self-authenticating and endowed with certainty, requiring no further principles to ground them. In similar fashion he looked for some principle or source in the spiritual life which could function in a similar way as an indubitable point of reference on which all particular and fallible decisions about God's will could rest. He considered that he had found such a principle in a particular kind of religious experience which Ignatius describes as 'consolation without preceding cause'.[10]

Rahner fastened on Ignatius' notion, and then interpreted it in his own way. He drew it into his philosophy of transcendence and interpreted the absence of preceding cause as the absence of a consciously perceived categorial object over against the person making the discernment. In this sense it is a question of a perception with a content but without an object. The content is transcendence itself, or more accurately the person as aware of transcendence and so as transcending any particular object. In fact Rahner specifies this content further: it is a question of an awareness of the existential tendency of the human spirit towards enjoying God in an eventual beatific vision.[11] In the case of the Ignatian Exercises, of course, it is an instance of a religious experience, and this grasp of transcendence is elevated by grace and suffused with a transcendental revelation of the divine. This is the way Rahner interprets a phrase of Ignatius where he talks about this experience drawing the soul 'entirely into love of His Divine Majesty'.[12]

Rahner's interpretation fits in very well with transcendental theology, but a prior question arises as to whether it is an accurate representation of Ignatian thought. Two shortcomings in his account have been picked out by subsequent Ignatian scholarship. For one thing, to define this unique kind of consolation as having a content without an object, though sometimes defensible, does not always fit the evidence of Ignatian sources, as a number of Ignatian experts have pointed out.[13] Secondly, Rahner's notion of this consolation as an unqualified self-authenticating certainty, analogous to the certainty of the first principles of logic, is not borne out by closer study of the Ignatian texts.[14] We will return to this point in more detail in the second main section of this article.

b) *Rahner on the Pre-Conceptual in Knowledge*

The sharp distinction which Rahner draws between the primary experience of consolation in transcendence and the implementation of this experience in individual decisions is one aspect of a larger issue in Rahner's philosophy of knowledge. Like Lonergan, he is anxious to distance himself from the rather rationalistic and deductivist scholasticism of an older generation, which both writers consider as excessively rigid and limited in perspective. Both authors, though each on very different premises, designate the old-style scholasticism as conceptualist. They wish to free up the process of reflection by grounding the conceptual on the pre-conceptual.

Building on his familiar schema of categorial and transcendental, Rahner developed a distinction between, on the one hand, 'reflexive consciousness', and, on the other, 'basic consciousness'.[15] Human knowledge, he tells us, is always 'bi-polar'.[16] At the objective pole there is reflexive consciousness, which corresponds to our ordinary notion of knowledge as something conceptual, categorial, explicit, or, as Rahner would say, 'thematic'. It is the field of clear premises and of deductive reasoning between propositions. It is also the field of Church doctrine and explicit faith.

Prior to this activity, however, and underlying it at its subjective pole, there is basic consciousness. As a prior awareness, basic consciousness is pre-conceptual. It is that grasp of the transcendental to which we have referred so often. As Rahner understands it, this grasp of transcendence comes about through an inarticulate and pre-conceptual grasp of oneself as a spiritual being, albeit an in-the-world being. To quote his own words:

> Firstly, there is among these forms of knowledge an *a priori*, unobjectified knowledge about oneself, and this is a basic condition of the spiritual subject in which it is present to itself and in which it has at the same time its transcendental ordination to the totality of possible objects of knowledge and of free choice.[17]

In this pre-conceptual grasp of self Rahner discovers a considerable store of knowledge. Notice that, unlike Lonergan, he uses the term 'knowledge' for this pre-conceptual grasp, but *ex hypothesi* it is a question of a non-thematic, inarticulate awareness, which only later reflexive consciousness can put into words. For example, in this grasp one is aware of the procedures of logic long before they can be expressed in a formal system. A young man in love, we are told, knows more about the meaning of love than any 'dried-up metaphysician' of the topic.[18] It is within this grasp of one's own self that Rahner locates our primary grasp of transcendence and of all that he eventually builds on that, including the notion of transcendental revelation, which, in turn, includes a non-objective awareness of God.

In all this I would wish to underline how this comprehensive form of knowledge is a function of consciousness in the sense of awareness of one's own self. Seeing so much weight placed on the subjective pole of knowledge, one can see how a case can be made that this emphasis has disturbed the balance between subjective and objective, between individual and outside world, between what we find in ourselves and what we need from others, not least from the life of the Church, its teachings and its sacraments. In Rahner's case I think the balance is weighted heavily on the side of the individual, at least in this context, with consequences often somewhat contrary to Rahner's own best instincts and intention, being in himself a man of the Church through and through.[19]

This in fact is the background to Rahner's discussion of the application of the principles of morality to particular situations. As in many other areas of theology, he here relativises the conclusions that follow deductively from these principles, since that is the whole field of propositional and reflexive consciousness which he has downgraded in favour of an appeal to the uniqueness of the individual. He has a good philosophical argument for that uniqueness in his famous essay, on formal existential ethics,[20] but he also claims that he is simply applying the model of decision-making as found in the election and discernment of spirits in the Ignatian Exercises.[21] In my view, Rahner's basic approach to particular decisions is more at home in the Ignatian Exercises than in the general field of morality, for Ignatius makes it clear that his election process applies only to matters that are morally neutral.[22] But a more fundamental reason for disagreeing with Rahner will appear from considering some principles from Lonergan and Crowe.

3. The Approach of Lonergan to the Pre-Conceptual

Parallel to Rahner's criticism of conceptualism, there is a critique by Lonergan on very different principles. For the Canadian his contrast, as he expresses it, between conceptualism and intellectualism goes to the heart of his entire philosophy of knowledge,[23] but I will take up just two points of contrast with the views of his German confrère which we have just described.

We might begin with the notion of consciousness. This is an important notion for both writers, and many of the things which Rahner writes about it could at first seem quite similar to Lonergan. In fact, however, the differences between them are profound and go back to how they understand that primal act of the human mind as described in *Insight* on the one hand and in *Spirit in the World* on the other.[24] What I have referred to as the primal act of the mind is the notion of being. In *Insight*, this notion is a question, where answers come from the unfolding process of understanding and judgment. In *Spirit in the World* the primary act is the pre-apprehension of being, the

Vorgriff in German. As in Lonergan, this is described at first as a question, but then as one containing its own answer. It is a judgment.[25]

This contrast in the two authors initiates, in my view, the fundamental difference between them that widened eventually into a gulf. The reason for this contrast lies, I believe, in two different views of the process of abstraction by which our concepts are formed – but I will not delay over that here.[26] It seems to this writer that, given the model of judgment with which he understands the pre-apprehension of being, Rahner's notion of human thinking too easily falls within the framework of a subject-object schema, even when he denies that there is an object. Consciousness for him covers not only what Lonergan calls consciousness but also what the latter calls introspection. Introspection for Lonergan is a subject taking the subject as an object. This helps explain why the whole notion of 'basic consciousness' for Rahner should come to be focused on the self as content and is a form of knowledge, knowledge of self.

Lonergan allows that such an activity does take place, but his name for it, as we have just seen, is not consciousness but introspection. Introspection in his system is the subject knowing the subject as object, and it is distinguished clearly from consciousness. Consciousness for Lonergan occurs when the subject is aware of the subject as subject. It is not, strictly speaking, a form of knowledge at all but of what he calls experience, inner experience. It is the subject's awareness of the subject, out of the corner of its eye as it were, while engaged in being aware of objects. In this view consciousness, in the strict sense of the term, is much more restricted in its scope. It is not properly described as an instance knowledge at all but as an infra-structure of knowledge, and so it leaves open a much wider field, to be filled eventually by the processes of knowledge, namely by acts of understanding and judging. As a consequence, consciousness alone is not capable of providing an answer to the demands of a pre-conceptual sphere in our knowledge of the world.

In Lonergan's philosophy concepts are not formed unconsciously. There is a pre-conceptual factor in the formation of each and every concept. Consciously we form our concepts in a particular way because of our understanding of the data presented to us by experience. That understanding occurs in an act of insight, which is then expressed in the concept. The concept, therefore, is secondary to the act of insight and dependent on it. In Rahner the pre-conceptual, while including an awareness of data, has a focus in the knower's self-identity; in Lonergan it is focused on the phantasm, namely on the data which experience presents for the consideration of our enquiring minds.

4. Crowe on Concrete Decisions

Rahner designed his notion of a formal existential ethics as a response to the discussion of Situation Ethics. Lonergan, as far as I know, has not addressed the problem in a systematic way, but the Boswell to his Johnson, Frederick Crowe, has done so in an article published in 1955 and recently republished in a collection of some of the author's essays.[27] This article poses the problem as one of application: how does one apply universal moral principles to particular cases?

The question, the writer tells us, is more complex than people realise,[28] but the hub of his solution turns on the role of understanding prior to any formulation of a moral obligation. Where Rahner presents such pre-conceptual understanding as basically an understanding of one's self in one's concrete individuality, Crowe, following Lonergan, sees it as a question of understanding one's situation, in other words, a question of insight into phantasms provided by one's experience of the outside world. Application is simply a further stage in this process of understanding, in which the intelligibility of the situation is grasped by the person.[29] He cites Aquinas, 'Our intellect needs to turn to phantasms, not only in acquiring knowledge, but also in using knowledge already acquired'.[30]

The point Crowe is making here is illustrated rather engagingly in the following paragraph, which pictures for us a vanished age.

> In religious life the imprudence of novices is proverbial. They live by a set of rules which they lack the wisdom to apply. Taught the necessity of silence they turn it into an absolute and are silent when the house burns down around them. Then they are taught not to be silent while the house burns down, and so by the addition of exceptions to the rules, and then of exceptions to the exceptions, they try to build up a code of rules which will be a complete guide to religious life. The task is necessary but achievement is hopeless; there is no possibility of a code that will cover every eventuality. In any case their need of a detailed code is only interim; it diminishes steadily as their understanding of the intelligible order of their new life grows to maturity. Then they will be able to formulate for themselves...the rules and exceptions to rules and exceptions to exceptions for which they once relied on their novice-master. They will do so by the light of intellect, natural and infused, formulating ever new practical judgments by grasping the intelligibility of ever new data. They have a principle of both permanence and adaptation.[31]

Applying this reflection to Ignatian discernment, one can see that this line of approach makes a lot of sense of the Third Time of Election in the Ignatian Exercises, a procedure which Rahner regarded as 'a deficient modality' of the Election process.[32] His begrudging assessment of it is not borne out by Ignatius' own practice, as witnessed in his Spiritual Diary, and stands in sharp contrast with the more positive assessment of this Third Time of Election by an Ignatian expert such as Jules Toner.[33]

5. The Experience of the Divine

A second issue in which the tension between transcendental and categorial comes to a head is that which concerns what Ignatius calls 'consolation without preceding cause'.[34] Rahner fastened on this notion as the king-pin of the whole discernment process, and tended to identify it with what Ignatius called First Time Election, transferring to the former the aspect of certainty proper to the latter.[35] On this he proceeded to carry out a kind of Heideggerian hermeneutic, by which he tried to present to us what Ignatius meant rather than what he actually said. Of course his account of what Ignatius really meant was inevitably coloured by the categories of Rahner's own approach. On this basis Rahner went on to develop his analogy between discernment and the ordinary procedures of logic and ontology. Just as logic depends on a primary experience of self-authenticating first principles, so Rahner saw the primary Ignatian experience endowed with a kind of certainty which did not quite fit Ignatius' description of consolation without preceding cause.[36]

Rahner bolstered this further by applying his philosophy of transcendental and categorial to the whole process, just as he had already done with the issues of moral decision.

Inevitably consolation without preceding cause was interpreted in terms of the transcendental, and this is how, as we have seen, he came to describe it as the grasp of a content without an object. Since it was presented as free of any categorial object, it was easier to attribute to it the kind of certainty claimed by Rahner. Rahner saw in all this a significant turn to the human subject, so that in his view Ignatius came to be cast in the role of pioneer of modernity four hundred years ahead of his time.

The corresponding experience in Lonergan's system is that described in chapter four of *Method in Theology*, namely the experience of the fulfilment of conscious intentionality in the dynamic state of falling in love with God. The account in that chapter gives us the paradigm for what constitutes religious experience for Lonergan, and it is certainly to be seen as an experience of grace. Lonergan explicitly identifies it with that operative grace which he had studied and expounded in traditional scholastic language in his doctoral dissertation.[37]

Rahner, however, speaks of something more than just of the experience of grace. Frequent under his pen comes the expression 'experience of God.' For him, in the present order of providence, the grasp of transcendence includes a grasp of God, and so he does not hesitate to speak of the primary Ignatian experience as a direct or immediate experience of God.[38] A good illustration of this will be found in Rahner's discussion of a famous passage is which Ignatius, writing to a lady, Teresa Rejadell, speaks of what is commonly taken to be an experience of consolation without preceding cause. Rahner clearly interprets it as a direct experience of God, even to the point that, using his brother Hugo's translation, he speaks of the experience's 'immediate origin from God' where the word 'immediate' is not found in Ignatius' original.[39]

At other times, doing better justice to the interdependence of transcendental and categorial, Rahner speaks of the immediacy he has in mind as a 'mediated immediacy'.[40] The main point of this latter expression is that God is not experienced as an object in the ordinary sense of the word. He is the term, in the sense of terminus, of the movement of transcendence. By this movement Rahner refers to the aspirations of our knowledge and freedom reaching out within us for an unknown term and fulfilment. This term is God, the goal of these aspirations. In one place he gives careful qualifications of his point of view. This goal, he tells us, 'is not experienced in itself but only in an unobjectified way within the experience of transcendence... It can never be approached directly or grasped immediately'.[41]

Rahner swings backwards and forwards between these two kinds of language. In his key essay on discernment,[42] the emphasis is on the uniqueness of the experience as a particular identifiable experience of God, in the light of which he interprets the Ignatian texts on consolation without preceding cause and First Time Election. Many readers of Rahner have followed him in this approach, failing to appreciate the qualifications of his view which in fact exist in his own mind and are explicitated elsewhere, as in the quotation just translated from the fourth volume of *Schriften zur Theologie*.

In contrast to Rahner's strong expressions of the experience of God, there is a striking reserve about such language that is characteristic of Lonergan. He speaks of an experience of grace, or an experience of the divine, but not of an experience of God. The reason for his reserve is well captured in the following quotation: 'While we do not in this life experience God, we do not know him apart from experience. We do not experience him, for God is not among the data of sense or the data of consciousness'.[43] There is one place in Lonergan's writings where the expression 'experience of God' has been found, namely in a lecture to a summer school on method in Toronto, 1969. There however the reference was clearly to the special case of consolation without preceding cause.[44]

Given this contrast in the two authors' usage of the phrase 'experience of God', one should bear in mind the differences in their understanding of experience itself. For Lonergan experience has the more precise meaning which comes to it from its context in his cognitional theory. It is the first level in the process of knowing, distinct from, and presupposed by, understanding and judging. Some of the implications of this more precise notion are illustrated by the quotation from him in the preceding paragraph. For Rahner the meaning is broader. He describes experience, *Erfahrung*, simply as a passivity, namely as 'the direct reception of an impression' coming to it from a reality 'outside our free control'.[45] However in Rahner's case the notion cannot be disassociated from his notion of God's presence on the analogy of formal causality. The inherent difficulty in this analogy will occupy us in our next section.

6. The Causality of Grace

In the background to the contrast between Rahner and Lonergan on the experience of God there is a divergence of interpretation on the theology of grace, which is radical and far-reaching. It is a question of how we understand the causality of God in the events of this world. Two kinds of causality are immediately relevant to our question, efficient causality and formal causality. Rahner has a problem about efficient causality. In his notion of it there remains a certain distance between cause and effect as a result of which it cannot do justice to the kind of immediacy which Christian sources find in our supernatural life. The implications of this point of view are far-reaching, since it helps to explain the preference Rahner accords throughout his system to formal and 'quasi-formal' causality; it is fundamental to his notion of the immediacy of God in grace, and for him it contains the ultimate explanation of the distinction between natural and supernatural.[46]

Of course Rahner knows perfectly well that, strictly speaking, God cannot be formal cause of any finite reality, but he is saved from that problem by the addition of the prefix 'quasi'. In the strictest sense of the term, hylemorphism here can only be an analogy, but one must question just how real is the intelligibility yielded by the analogy. Does Rahner not take away with the 'quasi' all that he has gained by the term 'formal'?

Lonergan travels a different path altogether. First of all, he is quite adamant in rejecting formal causality as a model for how Creator and creature come into union. He treats of the question in the context of the hypostatic union, but the principle is the same for the union with God in grace.[47] His basic difficulty with this model lies in that matter and form explain unity through the one principle's being in due proportion to the other; but between finite and infinite, between creature and Creator, there can be no proportion. Consequently the proposed analogy breaks down at the very point where it is meant to throw light. As Lonergan says sharply, 'The two cases are so utterly different that the only similarity between them lies in terminology'.[48] The two cases referred to are of course the union of finite and infinite on the one hand and that between matter and form on the other.

Then there is Lonergan's own approach to the presence of God in grace. This presence is clearly affirmed by him, and is a key feature of his notion of religious experience. The gift of the Spirit in Romans 5:5 is a favourite quotation in this context and marks, as he puts it, 'the entry of God into the life of men',[49] but to explain this presence he goes not to formal but to efficient causality. In his view there is no distance between efficient cause and its effect. Indeed he is confident that efficient causality gives us our main clue as to the very meaning of presence, deriving it, as he does, from the Aristotelian principle that causation is simply the relation of the effect with respect to the cause,[50] and so, as the Latin tag has it, *actio est in passo*.[51] Contrary to common sense notions, action is the presupposition of presence, not vice versa. The very meaning of action implies this presence of the cause in the effect, so that conversely the presence of the cause in the effect is central to the very meaning of presence as such.

Consequently, in Lonergan's philosophy, efficient causality, far from creating a problem for the notion of immediacy in presence, contains the very explanation of what such immediacy might mean. Through the efficient causality of God's love descending through all the levels of consciousness, the Holy Spirit is not only at work but is immediately present within us, with the result that, as Lonergan eloquently puts it, there is a charged field of love and meaning which pervades the world like a room filled with music.[52]

Finally, an account of Lonergan's notion of the experience of the divine would not be complete without underlining the role of feelings in his whole approach, for feelings figure so significantly in his notion of experience. The later Lonergan lays great stress on the role of feelings in our conscious life.[53] When we consider his schema of the four levels of consciousness, feelings fit into the first of these four, namely on the level of experience, but there is a special connection between first level and fourth level as feelings resonate with values and are integral to the way values are discovered in the first place.[54]

Clearly this mutual resonance is particularly relevant to the outpouring of the Holy Spirit which Paul speaks of in Romans 5:5. This gift of the Spirit leads directly to that supreme event on the fourth level of consciousness when the human being falls in love with God, an event that, in turn, inevitably overflows on human feeling and so constitutes the key role of affectivity in spirituality and mysticism.[55] Once you love God, says Lonergan, affectivity is of a single piece.[56]

Conclusion

Lonergan's own analogy for the union of Creator and creature is a complicated reflection on the meaning of contingent predications about an unchanging divinity.[57] For our purposes, however, it will be sufficient to rest the contrast between the two authors on their divergent notions of efficient causality, as already explained. Putting the two topics together, the notion of individual decisions and the notion of the experience of the divine, we get a striking indication of how the scholastic tradition is no strait-jacket, how a similarity on the surface can cover a wide diversity in both theology and philosophy. It is really only on that level that an ultimate judgment between the two authors is to be made.

We have seen how Rahner's principles lead to a number of problems. Implicit in our presentation is the suggestion that Lonergan's principles, when applied to the same issues, would avoid these problems. As regards the first topic treated, that of particular decisions, I think Lonergan's approach yields a much better appreciation of Ignatian discernment, validating more significantly the Third Time Election, and leading to a more restrained and careful application of the higher forms of Election.

As regards the topic of the experience of grace, I think Lonergan's more careful approach enables any one inspired by his principles to avoid the kind of problems which can arise from Rahner's perhaps over-emphatic presentation of the experience of God. In general one could describe this advantage as one based on a better balance between transcendental and categorial. In particular one notices that where Rahner's notion of the immediate presence of God pre-disposes him to an over-individualistic emphasis, Lonergan has striking statements that a modern notion of the human person has to be essentially communal,[58] and that religious experience is not solitary.[59] This leads eventually to a much less individualistic view of religious experience, to one better integrated into the concrete demands of ecclesial and sacramental life, and so to one better able to resist the secularising tendencies, independent of the Church, which Rahner's principles are sometimes felt to promote.

Notes

1   For example, Gordon Rixon, 'Lonergan and Mysticism', *Theological Studies* 62 (2002), pp. 479-97; Raymond Moloney, 'The Person as Subject of Spirituality in the Writings of Bernard Lonergan', *Milltown Studies* 45 (Summer 2000), pp. 66-80; Idem, 'The Spiritual Journey in the Writings of Bernard Lonergan', *Milltown Studies* 46 (Winter 2000), pp. 112-27.

2   For example, *FCF*, pp. 14-21, 51-55.

3   Rahner himself acknowledges the difficulty, for instance *FCF*, p. 139.

4   Endean, *Karl Rahner and Ignatian Spirituality*, p. 149. This work will be referred to below as *Ignatian Spirituality*.

5   'Religious Enthusiasm and the Experience of Grace', *TI* 16, p. 45.

6   Here the outstanding critic has been Hans Urs von Balthasar, *The Moment of Christian Witness*, San Francisco: Ignatius, 1994, pp. 100-113, 146-52.

7   *The Moment of Christian Witness*, p. 148.

8   'On the Question of a Formal Existential Ethic', *TI* 2, pp. 217-34.

9   *Ibid.*, p. 228.

10 St Ignatius, *Spiritual Exercises* #330.

11 '...the supernatural and immediate vision of God which according to Christian dogmatics is man's end and fulfilment,' *FCF*, p. 118.

12 Ignatius, *Spiritual Exercises* #330. I might add that Lonergan took over Rahner's notion of consolation without preceding cause and incorporated it into his own approach. This fact, however, is only incidental in relation to what comes later in this paper. See, *Method*, p. 106.

13 Jules Toner, *A Commentary on St Ignatius' Rules for the Discernment of Spirits*, St. Louis: Institute of Jesuit Sources, 1991, p. 249; Michael Ivens, *Understanding the Spiritual Exercises*, Leominster: Gracewing, 1998, p. 228; Endean, *Ignatian Spirituality*, p. 163.

14 Jules Toner, *Discerning God's Will: Ignatius of Loyola's Teaching on Christian Decision-Making*, St Louis: Institute of Jesuit Sources, 1991, p. 117; *A Commentary on St. Ignatius' Rules*, p. 245; Jean Governaire, *Quand Dieu entre à l'improviste*, Paris: Desclée, 1980, pp. 125-31.

15 E.g., 'The Development of Dogma', *TI* 1, pp. 63-65; 'Dogmatic Reflections on the Knowledge and Self-Consciousness of Christ', *TI* 5, p. 200.

16   'The Resurrection of the Body', *TI* 2, p. 208.

17   'Dogmatic Reflections', *TI* 5, pp. 200-201.

18   'The Development of Dogma', *TI* 1, p. 63.

19   The individualist tendency in Rahner has been noted by various critics from different perspectives, like Fergus Kerr, *Theology after Wittgenstein*, Oxford: Blackwell, 1966, p. 14; Jürgen Moltmann, *The Trinity and the Kingdom of God*, London: SCM, 1981, pp. 145ff.

20   'On the Question of a Formal Existential Ethics,' *TI* 2, p. 226.

21   *Ibid.*, pp. 231-232.

22   Ignatius, *Spiritual Exercises* #170.

23   Lonergan, *CWL*, 2 [*Verbum: Word and Idea in Aquinas*], 153 (original edition 1967). See also *CWL*, 4 [*Collection*], 91; also Editorial Note, *Ibid.*, p. 270 (original edition 1967).

24   *CWL*, 3 [Insight], (original edition 1957) and Rahner, *Spirit in the World*, London: Sheed & Ward, 1968.

25   *SW*, p. 61. See also *HW*, (1969), p. 35.

26   This matter is discussed in Bernard Lonergan, *Verbum: Word and Idea in Aquinas*, ed., David C. Burrell, London: Darton, Longman & Todd, 1968, Chapter 4, especially p. 163. For Rahner, see *SW*, Chapter 3. Note especially the latter's statement, 'Therefore the first acquisition of a quiddity (abstraction) takes place as a judgment'. *Ibid.*, p. 208, n. 20.

27   Fred Crowe, 'Universal Norms and the Concrete 'Operabile' in St Thomas Aquinas,' *Three Thomist Studies*, Boston: Boston College, 2000, pp. 3-69.

28   *Ibid.*, p. 6.

29   *Ibid.*, p. 27.

30   *De Veritate*, q. 18, a. 8, obj. 4, cited by Crowe, *Three Thomist Studies*, p. 29.

31   Crowe, *Three Thomist Studies*, p. 54.

32   Karl Rahner, *The Dynamic Element in the Church*, London: Burns & Oates, 1964, p. 105.

33   Toner, *Discerning God's Will*, pp. 257ff; 265ff.

34   Ignatius, *Spiritual Exercises*, ## 330 and 336. I will refer to this consolation as the primary or key Ignatian experience, following the example of Endean, *Ignatian Spirituality*, pp. 130-33.

35   *Ibid.*, #175.

36   Ignatius' description of this consolation as involving 'no deception' (*Spiritual Exercises* #336) is not the same thing as the

freedom from doubt which is attributed to First Time Election (*Ibid.* #175). Thus Toner, *Discerning God's Will*, p. 117; *A Commentary on St. Ignatius' Rules for the Discernment of Spirits*, p. 245.

37 *Method*, p. 107.

38 In Annotation 15 in the *Spiritual Exercises*, Ignatius himself uses the term 'immediate' of God's dealings with the retreatant, but to assume that this possibly loose use of language validates the technical sense of Rahner is to beg the question.

39 *The Dynamic Element in the Church*, p. 152. The question of this translation is well discussed by Endean, *Ignatian Spirituality*, pp. 161-64.

40 Rahner, *FCF*, pp. 83-86.

41 Karl Rahner, *Schriften zur Theologie*, Einsiedeln: Benziger, 1964, vol. 4, p. 73 in this writer's translation. Rahner's word for 'goal' in this context is 'das Woraufhin'. See *TI* 4, p. 52 for an alternative translation of the sentence.

42 *The Dynamic Element in the Church*, pp. 84-170.

43 Bernard Lonergan, Letter to Rocco Cacòpardo, 23 January 1968, cited by F. Crowe in a note in *The Lonergan Studies Newsletter* (September 2000), p. 7.

44 Bernard Lonergan, *The Method of Theology: Institute Given at Regis College, Toronto, July 7-18, 1969* (unpublished typescript of the Institute prepared from tapes by Nicholas Graham, Toronto: Lonergan Research Institute, 1984, p. 682.)

45 *Concise Theological Dictionary*, eds., Karl Rahner and Herbert Vorgrimler, London: Burns Oates, 1965, p. 162. In the background also is his notion of the emanation of sensibility from the human spirit, *SW*, pp. 253ff.

46 'The Concept of Mystery in Catholic Theology', *TI* 4, p. 66.

47 *CWL*, 7, pp. 116-21.

48 *Ibid.*, p. 121.

49 *A Second Collection: Papers by Bernard J.F. Lonergan*, eds., William Ryan and Bernard Tyrrell, Philadelphia: Westminister/London: Darton Longman & Todd, 1974, p. 130.

50 *CWL*, 1, pp. 68-69, (original edition 1971). Aquinas' expression of this truth is not exactly the same as Aristotle's, but it comes to the same thing, as Lonergan points out, *Ibid.*, pp. 68-73.

51 English: action is a reality in the recipient (of the action): Lonergan, *Collection*, p. 58.

52 *Method*, p. 290.
53 Raymond Moloney, 'The Person as Subject of Spirituality in the Writings of Bernard Lonergan', *Milltown Studies* 45 (Summer 2000), pp. 66-80, at pp. 71-73.
54 *Ibid.*, p. 79, citing *Method*, pp. 37-38 and p. 245.
55 Raymond Moloney, 'The Spiritual Journey in the Writings of Bernard Lonergan,' *Milltown Studies* 46 (Winter 2000), pp. 112-127, at pp. 119-20.
56 *Method in Theology*, p. 39.
57 *CWL*, 7, pp. 94-105.
58 Bernard Lonergan, *Philosophy of God and Theology: The Relationship between Philosophy of God and the Functional Specialty Systematics*, London: Darton Longman & Todd, 1973, p. 59.
59 *Method*, pp. 118-19.